Interlibrary Loan
in College Libraries

CLIP Note #16

Compiled by

Roxann Bustos
Assistant Head of Public Services
Reese Library
Augusta College

College Library Information Packet Committee
College Libraries Section
Association of College and Research Libraries
A Division of the American Library Association

ASSOCIATION OF
COLLEGE
& RESEARCH
LIBRARIES
A DIVISION OF THE
AMERICAN LIBRARY ASSOCIATION

Published by the Association of College and Research Libraries
A Division of the American Library Association
50 East Huron Street
Chicago, IL 60611-2795

ISBN: 0-8389-7652-2

This publication is printed on recycled paper with vegetable based ink.

Printed in the United States of America.

TABLE OF CONTENTS

INTERLIBRARY LOAN FORMS

Book/Journal Request Forms

Book Request Forms

Journal Request Forms

CLIP NOTES COMMITTEE

James Cubit, Chair
Williams College

Patricia S. Butcher
Trenton (NJ) State College

Carol F. Goodson
West Georgia College

Andrea C. Hoffman
Wheelock College

Lawrie Merz
Houghton College

Allen S. Morrill
Kansas City Art Institute

Karen A. Nuckolls
Skidmore College

INTRODUCTION

Objective:

The College Library Information Packet (CLIP) Notes series is published under the auspices of the College Libraries Section of the Association of College and Research Libraries to provide college and small university libraries with information and documentation on current library practices and procedures. "The basic premise underlying the program is that libraries throughout the nation are facing numerous challenges due to changing environments and that many of these libraries can benefit by knowing how similar institutions have resolved certain problems" (Morein, 1985, 226). This CLIP Note examines the critical topic of interlibrary loan (ILL).

Background:

The economic pressures experienced by libraries in recent years have had serious repercussions for interlibrary loan departments. With increasing materials costs and relatively static library budgets, library acquisitions have not been able to keep pace with patron demand, meaning interlibrary loan departments everywhere have been inundated with work. The widespread availability of CD-ROM database searching and Internet access to other library catalogs has added even more to this flood of work for interlibrary loan departments. A study of interlibrary loan activity in one university showed a 200% increase in ILLs between 1982 and 1990 (Farr, 1991, 42-3). A preliminary report on an OCLC Office of Research project showed tremendous growth in total ILL activity in academic libraries from 1978 to 1989, with an especially large increase in the late 1980's (Jul and Prabha, 1992, 13-4). This CLIP Note was initiated to gather information about how college and small university libraries are dealing with this increased demand.

The Model Interlibrary Loan Code for Regional, State, Local, or Other Special Groups of Libraries (1980) and the National Interlibrary Loan Code (1980) adopted by the Reference and Adult Services Division of the American Library Association are widely accepted as general guidelines for interlibrary loan policy.

Specific policies of individual libraries vary greatly, however, and the cooperative nature of interlibrary loan makes it essential that libraries have access to information about other libraries' interlibrary loan policies. The interlibrary loan staff of a library requesting material from another must know not only that the library has the material, but also whether or not it loans that type of material, if there are charges, etc. Directories of lending policies are available online on systems such as the OCLC Online Computer Library Center and have been published in hardcopy by consortia like the Washington Library Network. The Interlibrary Loan Policies Directory, by Leslie R. Morris and Sandra Chass Morris (1991) also provides brief statements of the lending policies of over 1,550 libraries.

Information about borrowing policies is most important for the patrons and staff of a library and is commonly outlined in a service brochure.

Selected statements of policy that include both lending and borrowing have been published in Reference and Online Services Handbook: Guidelines, Policies, and Procedures for Libraries edited by Bill Katz and Anne Clifford (1982). Virginia Boucher's Interlibrary Loan Practices Handbook (1984) also includes a sample policy and samples of other interlibrary loan documents, as well as an excellent discussion of interlibrary loan practice. The Association of Research Libraries SPEC (Systems and Procedures Exchange Center) Kit #127, Interlibrary Loan in ARL Libraries (1986) published interlibrary loan policies of selected research libraries.

This CLIP Note survey was undertaken to collect data on current interlibrary loan policy and practice in college and small university libraries and especially to see how these libraries are dealing with today's pressures on their interlibrary loan services.

Survey Procedure:

A proposal and draft survey document were reviewed by the CLIP Notes Committee of the College Libraries Section of ACRL. The final version of the questionnaire was distributed to 260 libraries in March 1992. The libraries that have agreed to participate in the CLIP Notes Program serve institutions with enrollments between 1,000 and 5,000 students that are designated as "Comprehensive Universities and Colleges I" or "Liberal Arts Colleges I" in A Classification of Institutions of Higher Education (Carnegie Foundation for the Advancement of Teaching, 1987). Four weeks after the original mailing, a follow-up letter was sent, and a second copy of the survey was sent to libraries requesting one.

A total of 190 of the 260 questionnaires were returned for a 73% response rate. Survey data were compiled using Paradox database manager software. The tabulated questionnaire with summaries of responses is included.

SURVEY RESULTS

General Information (Questions 1-13)

Eighty-five percent of the libraries responding belonged to privately supported colleges or universities. The average number of full-time equivalent students enrolled in the fall of 1991 was 1578.5, the average number of FTE librarians was 6.12, and the average number of FTE staff was 11.2 The average number of volumes per library was 220,484.9.

Interlibrary Loan Policies (Questions 21-30)

Seventy-two percent of the 189 responding libraries have some kind of written interlibrary loan policy. Some of these policies are over twenty years old, while the dates of others suggest that they were prepared expressly for the survey. Some policies are detailed documents covering all aspects of interlibrary borrowing and lending, while others are simple fact sheets listing lending parameters or one paragraph notices to patrons about borrowing restrictions.

Most policies are revised as needed, but 33 libraries reported that their policies are checked yearly and 18 every two years. The usual author of the ILL policy is the interlibrary loan supervisor, often assisted by others in the ILL department or by reference librarians, and frequently subject to approval by the library director. Most policies are based on the National ILL Code and are available and updated online.

Of the 52 libraries reporting no written interlibrary loan policy, 36 said that they intended to prepare one. In addition, 5 of the libraries with some type of written policy answered yes to question #28, indicating that they intended to develop more complete policies. Most respondents feel that it is important to have a written policy, with the most common reasons being to provide consistent, equitable service and to facilitate continuity during staff changes.

Staffing for Interlibrary Loan (Questions 14-16)

Seventy-three percent of responding libraries indicated that their interlibrary loan department is supervised by a professional librarian. Very few interlibrary loan supervisors (9.5%) work exclusively in interlibrary loan; the additional responsibilities of these supervisors are very diverse, covering the gamut of library duties. The average number of full-time equivalent staff involved in interlibrary loan is 1.71, with most of these being support staff. Many libraries, however, indicated that both professional librarians and student assistants are also involved in day-to-day ILL activities.

Interlibrary Loan Activity (Questions 17-20)

The fact that there is little standardization in ILL statistics kept by libraries makes it difficult to compare activity between libraries. Some libraries keep records of only loan requests sent out to other libraries, while others record only loan requests that were actually filled. Likewise some libraries count only loan requests received by their library, while others count only those they filled. There was a very wide range of number of loan requests sent out for the fiscal year 1990/91 with the average being 1955.67, while the average number filled was 1845.58. The average number of loan requests received from other libraries during the same time period averaged 2751.55 with the average number filled being 1802.49.

Cooperative Interlibrary Loan Agreements (questions 31-32)

Over 90% of responding libraries participate in some type of local, state or consortia ILL agreement. The most common networks are OCLC-affiliated, but there are a great variety of local and special interest groups (e.g. Christian Library Association Network) which include interlibrary loan agreements. Less than one third of the respondents report that their cooperative ILL agreements include reimbursement or net lender financial support, with most of these consisting of state library reimbursements for loans.

Interlibrary Lending (questions 33-47)

Most libraries accept either ALA forms, OCLC or fax transmission of ILL requests, with a little over half also accepting telephone requests. A growing number of libraries accept electronic mail submission of requests as well.

Almost all of the libraries responding will lend to any type of library, with school libraries being the type most likely to be excluded. Most libraries are willing to lend to areas outside the U.S., with Canada and Europe being the non-U.S. areas most often specified.

Forty-four percent of responding libraries said that they do not charge at all for interlibrary loans. Most of these libraries do not levy any fees for lending, but a few do charge for photocopies. Thirteen percent of the libraries charge all borrowers, while 43% charge some borrowers, such as out-of-state borrowers, non-reciprocal borrowers or corporate libraries. Charges for books range from $1.00 to $10.00 with an average charge of $6.24. Photocopy charges range from $.05/page to a flat $10.00 fee. Fax transmission charges range from $.25/page to a flat $10.00 fee.

Very few libraries have in-state, out-of-state, or consortia scales. Those that do are most apt to have reduced charges or no charges for certain types of libraries in-state, such as academic, while charging for other types, such as corporate. Out-of-state scales usually offer reduced or no fees for nearby states. Consortia scales give reduced or no fees for consortia members, while charging others.

By far the most common loan period is one month (54%), with 22-28 days (20.5%) and 15-21 days (13.5%) being the next most common periods. Ninety-three percent of libraries will renew loaned materials and only 6.5% charge other institutions overdue fines on ILL materials. The fines charged range from $.05/day to a $5.00 flat fee.

Over half the libraries responding will not lend periodicals, reference materials, software, fragile items, audio-visual materials or microforms. Other types of materials that some libraries will not lend include best sellers and art books.

Sixty-one percent of the libraries claim that the average time from their receipt of a request from another library to their sending an item is 24 hours. Another 38.5% have a turnaround time of 2-3 days.

The most common form of delivery for both books and photocopies is the U.S. Postal Service (98% of libraries); 48% use United Parcel Service. Seventy-seven percent of libraries responding also use fax for photocopies.

Interlibrary Borrowing (Questions 48-65)

Most libraries borrow books only for patrons affiliated with their institution. A few will not borrow books for undergraduates. About one third of the libraries will do ILL for "outside" patrons, either with the permission of the director or for a fee.

An increasing number of libraries (33%) are finding it necessary to restrict the number of requests a patron is permitted to submit. Some typical limits are five requests per day, per week or in process or 10-15 requests per semester. Most libraries require the patron to submit the request in person, ensuring that a librarian will be able to check it; some, in fact, require a librarian's signature on the form. In addition to phone, mail and fax, alternative submission methods accepted by some libraries include electronic mail and an online system request module.

Most libraries will borrow items which they own, but which are temporarily unavailable, even though this practice is discouraged by the Model Interlibrary Loan Code. Most libraries will also try to borrow recently published books.

Seventy-five percent of libraries say they do verify outgoing ILL citations. Many of the others only verify suspicious-looking citations because of lack of staff time.

Forty-four percent of libraries do not charge students for interlibrary loans; 53% do not charge faculty; and 57% do not charge staff. To compensate for cancelled periodical subscriptions, at least one library (see page 83) has adopted a policy of providing free interlibrary loan of articles in journals to which the library does not subscribe. Libraries that do charge their patrons most commonly pass on any charges levied by the lending library. A small number (13% for students) have a service charge ranging from $.50-5.00 or, for copies, a charge per copy, often equivalent to the copy cost at the library. Another small group only pass on charges over a specified amount (ranging from $1.00 to $20.00).

Almost all libraries will try to renew ILL materials for their patrons. About 41% of libraries charge their patrons overdue fines, sometimes passing along any charge from the lending library and sometimes charging the same fines as for their own books.

Many libraries do not have a separate Interlibrary Loan Office; the Circulation or Reference desk often serves as the ILL Office. Loan requests are most commonly discussed with patrons by a reference librarian or member of the interlibrary loan support staff. Methods used for restricting interlibrary loans include not only charging for loans or limiting the number of requests that may be submitted, but also requiring student requests to be signed by a faculty member and talking with patrons about excessive requests.

In responding to the question about publicizing the availability of interlibrary loan service, one librarian commented, "Are you kidding! Look at the volume we have now!" Nevertheless most libraries do have some publicity, commonly through bibliographic instruction and orientation, campus media, posters and handouts.

Interlibrary Loan Statistics (Questions 66-67)

Seventy-seven percent of libraries do use interlibrary loan information, at least minimally, for collection development purposes. The most common use is an examination of the copyright file for possible purchase of frequently requested periodicals. About one third of the libraries responding compile interlibrary loan statistics using a computer program. In addition to a network or college statistical program, some of the software programs used include SAVEIT, ILLFILE, ENABLE, ILL Express and First Choice. Some libraries use information from the statistical program for collection development purposes.

Summary

Several libraries added comments to their questionnaires indicating that they were finding written policies more important with increased ILL demand. For example:

> In the past year. . . we have already almost doubled our total number
> of ILL requests for the previous year, with three months left to go.
> This drastic increase in ILL activity has caused us to question previous
> policy (or the lack thereof) and to see the need of completely reeval-
> uating our ILL policy and procedures and preparing a written policy
> statement....

As libraries find their staffs taxed to the limit, they are often forced to place restrictions on services that were once freely available to all without question. When this happens, written policies can be a great help to uncertain library staff in sticky situations with unhappy or belligerent patrons. In today's complex interlibrary loan environment, written interlibrary loan policies are practically essential to ensure efficient, equitable service.

Description of Documents

Libraries were requested to submit copies of their interlibrary loan policies, even if brief or incomplete. A great variety of materials were sent ranging from a few sentences in a library handbook to very complete documents covering all aspects of interlibrary loan policy and procedure. Related documentation was also requested, including service brochures, request forms, ILL procedures documentation and cooperative agreements for consortia. From the great mass of material that was received, documents were selected for publication that provide examples which can help libraries in preparing and refining their own policies and service brochures.

REFERENCES

Boucher, Virginia. (1984). Interlibrary Loan Practices Handbook. Chicago: American Library Association.

Carnegie Council on Policy Studies in Higher Education. (1987). A Classification of Higher Education, rev. ed. Berkeley, California: The Carnegie Foundation for the Advancement of Teaching.

Farr, Marianne and Barry Brown. (1991). Explosive ILL Growth at The University of Montana: A Case Study. Journal of Interlibrary Loan & Information Supply 2(2), 41-54.

Jul, Erik and Chandra Prabha. (1992). Office of Research project will determine costs, work flows, and usage data on ILL and document delivery. OCLC Newsletter. 199, 12-15.

Katz, Bill and Anne Clifford. (1982). Reference and Online Services Handbook: Guidelines, Policies, and Procedures for Libraries. New York: Neal-Schuman Publishers, Inc.

Morein, P. Grady. (1985). What is a CLIP note? College and Research Libraries News 46, 226-229.

Morris, Leslie R. and Sandra Chass Morris. (1991). Interlibrary Loan Policies Directory. New York: Neal-Schuman Publishers.

Office of Management Studies, Association of Research Libraries. (1986) Interlibrary Loan in ARL Libraries, SPEC Kit 127. Washington: Association of Research Libraries.

Schoen, David M. and Leslie R. Morris. (1990). Interlibrary Loan Policies: Data from the Interlibrary Loan Policies Directory. Journal of Interlibrary Loan & Information Supply, 1, 101-8.

WLN Interlibrary Loan Policies Directory. (1991). Lacey, WA: WLN.

CLIP NOTE SURVEY RESULTS

This survey is designed to gather information about interlibrary loan policy and practices in academic libraries. Please include any explanatory comments you feel would be helpful.

GENERAL INFORMATION

1) Institution name_____

190 responses

___29___ public
___161___ private

One library gave no responses past this point, "due to staff cuts."

2) Address _____

_____

_____

3) Name of respondent_____

4) Title_____

5) Telephone Number (____)_____

LIBRARY PROFILE (Fiscal year 1990/91)

6) If your records cover a period different from July 1, 1990-June 30, 1991, please indicate the period used_____

7) Number of full-time equivalent (FTE) students enrolled (Fall 1991)_____
188 responses; Range 375-5000; Mean 1805.28; Median 1578.5

8) Number of full-time equivalent (FTE) librarians (Fall 1991)_____
187 responses; Range 1-18.5; Mean 6.12; Median 5

9) Number of full-time equivalent (FTE) on library staff, not including student assistants (Fall 1991)_____*184 responses; Range 2-55.4; Mean 11.2; Median 8.45*

10) Total library expenditures(1990/91)_____
179 responses; Range $42,000-3,814,728; Mean $740,271.90; Median $552,267.90

11) Total book expenditures(1990/91)_____
183 responses; Range $3,316-1,309,883; Mean $161,746.31; Median $111,696.00

12) Number of volumes in library_____
187 responses; Range 46,852-1,033,183; Mean 220,484.9; Median 114,679

13) Number of current periodical subscriptions_____
   187 responses; Range 251-77,735; Mean 1576.41; Median 992

INTERLIBRARY LOAN PROFILE

14) Total number of full-time equivalent staff (FTE) involved in interlibrary
   loan_____ *165 responses; Range .25-10; Mean 1.71*

   _____number of professional librarians   *129 responses; Range 0-3; Mean .91*

   _____number of support staff   *143 responses; Range 0-4; Mean 1.14*

   _____number of student assistants   *137 responses; Range 0-10; Mean 2.22*

   _____others; please explain: *3 responses (e.g. volunteers, intern, circulation
                                      students who assist intermittantly with ILL)*

15) The person who supervises your interlibrary loan department is:

   189 responses

   __138__professional librarian
   __50__support staff
   __0__a student assistant
   __1__other; please explain briefly: *e.g. administrative*

16) The person who supervises your interlibrary loan department:

   148 responses

   __14__works exclusively in interlibrary loan
   __134__has other responsibilities (please describe briefly other responsibilities
   and estimate % of time spent on interlibrary loan):
   *Range .25%-97%; Mean 39.56% (other responsibilities very
   diverse--e.g. cataloging, circulation, collection development, archivist, science
   librarian, government documents, etc.--most common response: reference)*

17) Number of interlibrary loan requests sent to other libraries during the fiscal year
   1990/91 _____*156 responses; Range 34-7454; Mean 1955.67*

18) Number of interlibrary loan requests filled by other libraries during the fiscal year
   1990/91 _____*178 responses; Range 31-8217; Mean 1845.58*

19) Number of interlibrary loan requests received from other libraries during the fiscal
   year 1990/91 _____*150 responses; Range 0-10,850; Mean 2751.55*

20) Number of interlibrary loans filled for other libraries during the fiscal year
   1990/91 _____*178 responses; Range 0-9583; Mean 1802.49*

INTERLIBRARY LOAN POLICY

21) Do you have a written interlibrary loan policy?

   189 responses

   __137__yes (Please include a copy, even if brief or incomplete)
   __52__no (If no, skip to #28)

22) When was the policy written?_____
   115 responses; Range 1969-1992

23) How often is it revised?

134 responses

        _2_ never
      _33_ yearly
      _18_ every two years
      _80_ other; please specify: *e.g. as needed, occasionally, 2 times in 14 years*

24) Who wrote the policy? (check all that apply)

136 responses

       _46_ library director
     _104_ interlibrary loan supervisor
      _10_ library committee
      _35_ other; please specify: *e.g. reference staff, head of public services, who knows?*

25) Is it based on the National Interlibrary Loan Code, endorsed by the American Library Association, 1980?

134 responses

     _112_ yes
      _20_ no
         (2 "other" responses: does not duplicate it nor does it contradict it; complements it)

26) Is your policy available and updated online (e.g. OCLC Name-Address Directory)?

131 responses

     _105_ yes
      _26_ no

27) Which of the following does your policy cover? (check all that apply)

135 responses

_91_	interlibrary borrowing	_104_	interlibrary lending
_98_	clientele served	_65_	libraries served
_94_	materials borrowed	_116_	materials lent
_101_	charges	_114_	loan period
_70_	time involved	_112_	charges
_68_	copyright restrictions	_70_	fax policy

Comments:

28) If you do not have an interlibrary loan policy, do you intend to prepare one?

57 responses

     _41_ yes
     _16_ no

29) How important is it in your opinion, to have a written interlibrary loan policy?

182 responses

Not important				Very important
5	4	3	2	1
(2)	*(16)*	*(21)*	*(41)*	*(102)*

30) Please explain briefly why a written interlibrary loan policy is important to your library: *(e.g. Continuity, consistency of service, to give guidance to support staff, helps in decision-making in gray areas)*

COOPERATIVE INTERLIBRARY LOAN AGREEMENTS

31) Is your library a participant in any local, state, or consortia ILL agreements?

185 responses

     18 no (Skip to question #33)
     167 yes
     (Please include a copy of agreements)

Please check those that apply, giving names.
     111 local:
     100 state:
     126 consortia:

32) Do any of these agreements include reimbursement/net lender financial support?

166 responses

     112 no
     54 yes

Please explain briefly: *e.g. State or regional library reimbursement*

INTERLIBRARY LENDING

33) What transmission methods do you accept? (check all that apply)

189 responses

     188 ALA forms
     179 OCLC
     102 telephone
     160 fax
     2 telex
     1 RLIN
     34 electronic mail
     28 other; please specify: *e.g. hand carried, WLN, written letter,*
                                      DOCLINE

34) To whom do you lend ILL materials? (check all that apply)

188 responses

     187 academic libraries
     187 community and technical college libraries
     186 public libraries
     170 school libraries
     180 corporate libraries
     184 federal and state libraries
     40 other; please specify: *e.g. hospitals, historical societies, prisons,*
                                museums, seminaries, monastic communities, any OCLC

35) To what areas outside of the U.S. do you lend?

141 responses

8	Africa	*14*	Central and South America
8	Asia	*60*	Europe
11	Australia		
81	Canada	*76*	all of the above

36) Do you charge for interlibrary lending?

187 responses

     __82__ no, for all borrowers
     __24__ yes, for all borrowers
     __81__ yes, for the following (describe briefly)
         (e.g. out-of-state, non-reciprocal, corporate libraries)

37) If you charge, please list charges for:

     Books____*23 responses; range $1.00-10.00; mean $6.24*
     Photocopies____*79 responses; range $.05/p-$10.00; mean $2.88*
     Hard copies from microforms____*49 responses; range $.10/p-$10.00;*
                      mean $3.32
     Fax transmission____*34 responses; range $.25/p-$10.00; mean $3.51*
     Other formats (explain)____*3 responses; (ERIC fiche to fiche, A/V)*

38) Names of groups/consortia for which you waive fees:
     (e.g. OCLC consortia, Oberlin Group, in-state colleges, reciprocal institutions)

39) Do you have an in-state scale?   *153 responses*
     __143__ no
     __10__ yes; please describe: *e.g. free to academic and penitentiary libraries,*
                          postage for public and school libraries

40) Do you have an out-of-state scale?   *154 responses*
     __139__ no
     __15__ yes; please describe: *e.g. free to NC, SC and GA libraries, charge*
                          for others

41) Do you have a consortia scale?   *152 responses*
     __139__ no
     __13__ yes; please describe: *e.g. no charge for Minitex or Oberlin group*
                          libraries, charge for others

42) What is your regular interlibrary loan period?

185 responses

     __2__ 1-7 days
     __5__ 8-14 days
     __25__ 15-21 days
     __38__ 22-28 days
     __100__ one month
     __15__ longer than one month
           how long____*Range 35 days-16 weeks to faculty*

43) Will you renew loaned materials?   *187 responses*
     __13__ no
     __174__ yes
        for how long?____*Range 1 week-1 month*

44) Do you charge other institutions overdue fines on ILL materials?

183 responses

     __164__ no
     __12__ yes
        how much?____*Range $.05/day-$5.00 flat fee*

45) Check any of the following items that you will __NOT__ loan:

188 responses

- _160_ periodicals
- _160_ reference materials
- _51_ newly published materials
- _31_ dissertations
- _50_ theses
- _35_ government documents
- _50_ local history
- _44_ genealogical materials
- _91_ manuscripts
- _27_ oversized items
- _137_ fragile items
- _115_ microfilm
- _114_ microfiche
- _135_ audio-visual materials
- _140_ software
- _96_ realia
- _60_ other; please specify: *e.g. archival materials, rare books, special collections, art books, best sellers, juvenile books, cookbooks, student papers*

46) What is the average time from your receipt of a request from another library to your sending of the requested item? *187 responses*
- _115_ 24 hours
- _72_ 2-3 days
- _4_ 4-5 days
- _0_ 6-7 days
- _1_ longer than 7 days

47) What modes of delivery do you employ? Check all that apply.

186 responses

COPIES	BOOKS	
_183_	_174_	U.S. Postal Service
_32_	_91_	United Parcel Service
_92_	_82_	Local shuttle
_145_		FAX
_19_	_21_	other

please specify:
e.g. Federal Express, statewide delivery service

INTERLIBRARY BORROWING

48) Do you borrow materials for all library patrons?

187 responses

- _82_ yes
- _105_ no

if not, who is excluded? *e.g. patrons not affiliated with the institution, alumni, those who don't pay ILL fines, undergraduates (if there is a charge or without faculty permission)*

49) Do you do ILL for an "outside" patron by special arrangements?
179 responses

    _120_ no
      _59_ yes; please explain circumstances: *e.g. for a fee ($1.00-$10.00),*
                  alumni, board of trustees, emeritus faculty, permission of the
                  director, government documents, grant obligations

50) Do you limit the number of requests per patron?   *183 responses*
    _122_ no
      _61_ yes
    if yes, what is the limit? *Range 3-30 per topic, per day, per semester;*

51) Do you permit patrons to submit requests (check all that apply)
189 responses

    _188_ in person
      _88_ by phone
    _113_ by mail
      _69_ by fax
      _22_ other; please explain: *e.g. Bitnet, E-mail, marked copy of Dialog*
             search, online system request module

52) Will you borrow materials owned by your library, but temporarily unavailable (checked out, being bound, etc.)?   *172 responses*
      _38_ no
    _134_ yes/under certain circumstances; please explain: *e.g. at bindery, lost,*
          faculty need, dire need, recall not heeded, missing pages

53) Will you borrow recently published (in-print) books?
184 responses

       _8_ no
    _152_ yes
      _24_ under certain circumstances; please explain: *e.g. academic rather than*
          recreational need, not within our collection scope, evaluation for
          purchase, can't purchase in time for patron need, faculty request

54) Do you verify outgoing ILL citations?   *187 responses*
    _141_ yes
      _46_ no; please explain why not: *e.g. not enough time, not enough staff,*
          most are O.K., only verify those that look suspicious

55) Do you charge your students for interlibrary loan?   *187 responses*
      _83_ no
      _70_ pass on charges
      _18_ pass on charges over the amount of _$1.00-20.00_
      _24_ service charge
          how much? *e.g. $.50-1.00/book; $.10-.25/p, $1.00-2.50 for photo-*
          copies, "copy costs here"

56) Do you charge faculty for interlibrary loan?   *187 responses*
      _99_ no
      _63_ pass on charges
      _16_ pass on charges over the amount of _$1.00-15.00; $20/yr._
      _17_ service charge
          how much? *e.g. $.50-5.00 or $.10-.25/p for photocopies*

57) Do you charge staff for interlibrary loan?   *187 responses*
      _104_ no
       _60_ pass on charges
       _15_ pass on charges over the amount of _$1.00-15.00; $20.00/yr._
       _16_ service charge
          how much? _$.50-5.00 or $.10-.25/p for photocopies_

58) Do you try to renew ILL materials for your patrons?   *180 responses*
       _5_ no
     _175_ yes

59) Do you charge your patrons overdue fines on ILL materials? *179 responses*
     _106_ no
      _73_ yes
        how much? *e.g. $.05-5.00/day; pass on lending library's fines; same
          as our own books*

60) Do you have an interlibrary loan office accessible to the public?
                                              187 responses
     _147_ yes
      _40_ no

61) Where is the interlibrary office located?   *182 responses*
      _54_ Reference Desk
      _44_ Circulation Desk
      _82_ Other; describe briefly: *e.g.lobby area, technical services, etc.*

62) Who discusses interlibrary loan requests with patrons?
                                           188 responses
     _166_ reference librarian
      _92_ other professional librarian(s)
     _129_ interlibrary loan support staff
      _37_ student assistant(s)
      _22_ other
        please specify: *e.g. circulation staff, no one*

63) Do you have any methods to restrict interlibrary borrowing other than charging or limiting the number of requests?   *182 responses*
     _150_ no
      _32_ yes; please explain: *e.g. copyright limit, encourage use of local libraries, non-seniors must get faculty to sign forms, talk to patrons about excessive requests, screen requests for appropriateness to curriculum*

64) Do you publicize the availability of interlibrary loan service to your patrons?
                                           188 responses
      _24_ no (If not, skip to #66)
     _164_ yes

65) If you do publicize interlibrary loan service, please describe briefly the methods you use: *e.g. bibliographic instruction, orientations, brochures, handbooks, newsletters, campus media, E-mail, reference interviews, bulletin board, posters, signs*

Please submit samples of any publicity materials (service brochures, etc.) you produce.

66) Do you use interlibrary loan information for collection development purposes?

181 responses

    _42_ no
    _139_ yes

        if yes, please briefly describe how: *e.g. collection development librarian examines copyright file, acquisition librarian gets copies of all requests, if classic we order, frequently-requested items considered for purchase, if we seem deficient in an area based on student requests we actively purchase in that area*

67) Do you use any computer programs (software packages) to collect interlibrary loan data and statistics?

183 responses

    _120_ no
    _63_ yes

        if yes, please list the name(s) of the package(s): *e.g. SAVEIT, PLANPERFECT, PFS, ILLFILE, ENABLE, ILL Express, Planning Assistant, First Choice, OCLC ILL statistical package, program set up by college, Lotus 1-2-3, DBase, Quattro Pro, Apple Works, Alpha 4*

Additional comments would be appreciated. Please attach a separate sheet to this survey for comments.

PLEASE ENCLOSE A COPY OF YOUR INTERLIBRARY LOAN POLICY AND ANY RELATED DOCUMENTS SUCH AS SERVICE BROCHURES, REQUEST FORMS, ILL PROCEDURES DOCUMENTATION AND COOPERATIVE AGREEMENTS FOR CONSORTIA, ETC.

THANK YOU VERY MUCH FOR YOUR COOPERATION!

MODEL AND NATIONAL INTERLIBRARY LOAN CODES

Model Interlibrary Loan Code for Regional, State, Local, or Other Special Groups of Libraries

Endorsed by Reference and Adult Services Division
Board of Directors, New York, June 1980.

PREFACE

The "Model Interlibrary Loan Code for Regional, State, Local or Other Special Groups of Libraries" is intended to provide guidelines for any group of libraries interested in developing an interlibrary loan code to meet special needs. The Model Code, while complementing the "National Interlibrary Loan Code, 1980," allows libraries more flexibility and creativity in satisfying interlibrary loan needs in a specific situation.

The Model Code is designed to provide a framework for cooperation. Since it is recognized that most networks and consortia can be more liberal in loaning materials, the Model Code has fewer restrictions than the National Code. All libraries in a network or consortium should participate in developing an interlibrary loan code. Each section of the code should be discussed and should be expanded or modified, if necessary, for local use. The bracketed sections of the Model Code indicate specific areas where local information may be necessary. Libraries are encouraged to put as few restrictions as possible on the exchange of materials.

The use of interlibrary loan service is becoming increasingly important to libraries committed to providing a high level of service to their clientele. In *A Commitment to Information Services: Developmental Guidelines, 1979*, the Reference and Adult Services Division emphasizes the importance of considering "the needs and interests of all users, including children, young adults, adults ...." Interlibrary loan is a service that should be publicized and provided to all members of the library's clientele.

A strong interlibrary loan network within a local, state, or regional jurisdiction should be the primary source of interlibrary loan materials for all libraries. Only after all of these resources have been exhausted should a library request material outside of these arrangements. In making outside requests, the "National Interlibrary Loan Code, 1980," and the *Interlibrary Loan Procedure Manual*[2] should be followed. This approach will distribute the burden of requests more equitably and provide better service for all libraries.

Model Interlibrary Loan Code for Regional, State, Local, or Other Special Groups of Libraries

This code is a voluntary agreement adopted by _____ _____[system, consortium, network, etc.] on _____ [date] to govern interlibrary lending among libraries in _____[metropolitan area, region, state, system, network, consortium, etc.]

INTRODUCTION

Interlibrary loan service is essential to the vitality of libraries of all types and sizes as a means of greatly expanding the range of materials available to users. Lending between libraries is in the public interest and should be encouraged. This code is intended to make interlibrary loan policies among those libraries adopting it as liberal and as easy to apply as possible. Interlibrary loan should serve as an adjunct to, not a substitute for, collection development. When resources within the region have been exhausted, loan requests to more distant libraries would then conform to the provisions of the "National Interlibrary Loan Code, 1980."

I. **Definition**

An interlibrary loan is a transaction in which library material, or a copy of the material, is made available by one library to another upon request.

II. **Purpose**

The purpose of interlibrary loan as defined in this code is to obtain library material not available in the local library.

III. **Scope**

Under the terms of this agreement, it is permissible to request on interlibrary loan any type of library material [except . . . .].

IV. **Responsibilities of Borrowing Libraries**

A. Each library should provide the resources to meet the ordinary needs and interests of its primary clientele. Material requested from another library under this code should generally be limited to those items that do not conform to the library's collection development policy or for which there is no recurring demand.

B. Borrowing libraries should make every effort to exhaust their own resources before resorting to interlibrary loans.

C. The interlibrary loan staff of each library should be familiar with, and use, relevant interlibrary loan documents and aids including _____
_____. [List here pertinent interlibrary loan codes, interlibrary loan procedure manuals, and bibliographic tools and services.]

D. Each library should inform its users of the purpose of interlibrary loan and of the library's interlibrary borrowing policy. Any member of the borrowing library's clientele should be eligible for interlibrary loan.

E. The borrowing library is responsible for compliance with the copyright law (Title 17, U.S. Code) and its accompanying guidelines, and should inform its users of the applicable portions of the law. An indication of compliance must be provided with all copy requests.

F. Requested material must be described as completely and accurately as possible following accepted bibliographic practice. If an item cannot be verified, the statement "cannot verify" should be included along with information about the original source of citation. [Variations in accepted bibliographic practice may be referred to here.]

G. Requests should be routed through channels established by libraries participating in this agreement. These channels are outlined in _____
[List here specific documents outlining agreed-upon channels.]

H. Standard interlibrary loan formats should be used for all requests, regardless of the means of transmission. [Variations from standard interlibrary loan formats may be referred to here.]

I. The safety of borrowed materials is the responsibility of the borrowing library from the time the material leaves the lending library until it is received by the lending library. The borrowing library is responsible for packaging the material so as to ensure its return in good condition. If damage or loss occurs, the borrowing library must meet all costs of repair or replacement, in accordance with the preferences of the lending library.

J. The borrowing library and its users must comply with the conditions of loan established by the lending library. Unless specifically forbidden by the lending library, copying by the borrowing library is permitted provided that it is in accordance with the copyright law and no damage to the original volume will result.

K. The borrowing library should encourage library users to travel to other libraries for on-site access to material when extensive use of a collection is required or the nature of the material requires special handling. The borrowing library should assist the user in making the necessary arrangements.

V. **Responsibilities of Lending Libraries**

A. The decision to loan material is at the discretion of the lending library. Each library is encouraged, however, to interpret as generously as possible its own lending policy with due consideration to the interests of its primary clientele.

B. A statement of interlibrary loan policy should be made available upon request and should be on file in the state library [or other appropriate agency].

C. The lending library should process requests promptly. [A specific number of days for processing may be inserted here.] Conditions of loan should be stated clearly and material should be packaged carefully. The lending library should notify the borrowing library when unable to fill a request, stating the reason for not filling the request.

D. A lending library is responsible for informing any borrowing library of its apparent failure to follow the provisions of this code.

VI. **Expenses**

A. The borrowing library should be prepared to assume any costs charged by the lending library and should attempt to anticipate charges and authorize them on the initial request. [List here any documents referring to charging policies.]

B. If the charges are more than nominal and not authorized by the borrowing library, the lending library should inform the requesting library and ask for authorization to proceed.

VII. **Duration of Loan**

A. The duration of loan, unless otherwise specified by the lending library, is the period of time the item may remain with the borrowing library disregarding the time spent in transit.

B. Interlibrary loan material should be returned promptly.

C. A renewal request should be sent in time to reach the lending library not later than the due date. If the lending library does not respond, it will be assumed that renewal, for the same period as the original loan, is granted.

D. All material on loan is subject to immediate recall, and the borrowing library should comply promptly.

VIII. **Violation of Code**

Each library is responsible for maintaining the provisions of this code in good faith.

National Interlibrary Loan Code, 1980

Adopted by Reference and Adult Services Division
Board of Directors, New York, 1980.

INTRODUCTION

Interlibrary loan is essential to the vitality of libraries of all types and sizes and is a means by which a wide range of material can be made available to users. This code is designed primarily to regulate lending relations between research libraries and between libraries operating outside networks or consortia. It is recognized that through specific agreements, libraries organized geographically, by mutual subject interest, or other bases will have developed codes of their own. It is not the intent of this code to prescribe the nature of interlibrary lending under such arrangements. (See "Model Interlibrary Loan Code for Regional, State, Local, or Other Special Groups of Libraries.")[1]

The effectiveness of a national system of interlibrary lending is directly related to the equitable distribution of costs among all the libraries involved. Interlibrary loan is an adjunct to, not a substitute for, collection development in individual libraries. Requests to national and research libraries or requests beyond networks and consortia should only be made after local, state, and regional sources have been exhausted. It is understood that every library must maintain an appropriate balance between resource sharing and responsibility to its primary clientele.

This national code contains general guidelines for the borrowing and lending of library material. Details of procedures to be used in implementing the code will be found in the *Interlibrary Loan Procedure Manual* published by the American Library Association.[2] All libraries participating in interlibrary loan should have copies of this publication and should follow these recommendations. The manual also provides information on international interlibrary loan.

The Reference and Adult Services Division, acting for the American Library Association in its adoption of this code, recognizes that the exchange of material between libraries is an important element in the provision of library service and believes it to be in the public interest to encourage such an exchange.

I   Definition

An interlibrary loan is a transaction in which library material, or a copy of the material, is made available by one library to another upon request.

II.   Purpose

The purpose of interlibrary loan as defined in this code is to obtain, for research and serious study, library material not available through local, state, or regional libraries.

III.   Scope

A. A loan or a copy of any material may be requested from another library in accordance with the published lending policy of that library. The lending library will decide in each case whether a particular item can be provided.

B. Most libraries will not ordinarily lend the following types of materials:
1. Rare or valuable material, including manuscripts;
2. Bulky or fragile items that are difficult or expensive to ship;
3. Material in high demand at the lending library;
4. Material with local circulation restrictions;
5. Unique material that would

be difficult or impossible to replace.

IV. **Responsibilities of Borrowing Libraries**

A. Each library should provide the resources to meet the study, instructional, informational, and normal research needs of its primary clientele. This can be accomplished through its own collection or through local, state, or regional cooperative resource-sharing agreements. Material requested from another library under this code should generally be limited to those items that do not conform to the library's collection development policy and for which there is no recurring demand.

B. The interlibrary loan staff of each library should be familiar with, and use, relevant interlibrary loan documents and aids. These include this code, the *Interlibrary Loan Procedure Manual*, lending policies of the major research libraries, and standard bibliographic tools and services.

C. Each library should inform its users of the purpose of interlibrary loan and of the library's interlibrary borrowing policy.

D. The borrowing library is responsible for compliance with the copyright law (Title 17, U.S. Code) and its accompanying guidelines, and should inform its users of the applicable portions of the law. An indication of compliance must be provided with all copy requests.

E. Requested material must be described completely and accurately following accepted bibliographic practice as outlined in the current *Interlibrary Loan Procedure Manual*. If the item cannot be verified, the statement "cannot verify" should be included along with complete information as to the original source of the citation.

F. The borrowing library should carefully screen all requests for loans and reject any that do not conform to this code.

G. Standard bibliographic tools, such as union catalogs, computerized data bases, and other listing services, should be used in determining the location of material. Care should be taken to avoid concentrating the burden of requests on a few libraries.

H. Standard interlibrary loan formats should be used for all requests, regardless of the means of transmission.

I. The safety of borrowed material is the responsibility of the borrowing library from the time the material leaves the lending library until it is received by the lending library. The borrowing library is responsible for packaging the material so as to ensure its return in good condition. If damage or loss occurs, the borrowing library must meet all costs of repair or replacement, in accordance with the preference of the lending library.

J. The borrowing library and its users must comply with the conditions of loan established by the lending library. Unless specifically forbidden by the lending library, copying by the borrowing library is permitted provided that it is in accordance with the copyright law and no damage to the original material will result.

K. The borrowing library should encourage library users to travel to other libraries for on-site access to material when extensive use of a collection is required or the nature of the material requires special handling. The borrowing library should assist the user in making the necessary arrangements.

V. **Responsibilities of Lending Libraries.**

A. The decision to loan material is at the discretion of the lending library. Each library is encouraged, however, to interpret as generously as possible its own lending policy with due consideration to the interests of its primary clientele.

B. A statement of interlibrary loan policy and charges should be made available upon request.

C. The lending library should process requests promptly. Conditions of loan should be stated clearly and material should be packaged carefully. The lending library should notify the borrowing library when unable to fill a request, stating the reason for not filling the request.

D. A lending library is responsible for informing any borrowing library of its apparent failure to follow the provisions of this code.

VI. Expenses

A. The borrowing library assumes responsibility for all costs charged by the lending library, including transportation, insurance, copying, and any service charges. The borrowing library should try to anticipate charges and authorize them on the original request.

B. It is recommended that nominal costs, such as postage, be absorbed by the lending library.

C. If the charges are more than nominal and not authorized by the borrowing library, the lending library should inform the requesting library and ask for authorization to proceed.

VII. Duration of Loan

A. The duration of loan, unless otherwise specified by the lending library, is the period of time the item may remain with the borrowing library disregarding the time spent in transit.

B. Interlibrary loan material should be returned promptly.

C. The borrowing library should ask for renewals only in unusual circumstances. The renewal request should be sent in time to reach the lending library no later than the date due. If the lending library does not respond, it will be assumed that renewal, for the same period as the original loan, is granted.

D. All material on loan is subject to immediate recall, and the borrowing library should comply promptly.

VIII. Violation of Code

Continued disregard of any provision of this code is sufficient reason for suspension of borrowing privileges.

INTERLIBRARY LOAN POLICIES
COMPLETE POLICIES

INTERLIBRARY LOAN POLICY

PURPOSE OF INTERLIBRARY LOAN

Purpose of Interlibrary Loan services is to provide access for
our patrons to materials not found in Adams State College
Library, and as a resource for materials from our collection to
all eligible requesting libraries. ASC Library maintains a
working relationship with other libraries in an effort to
efficiently share resources. These working relationships are
regulated by the Interlibrary Loan Code, and the policies and
procedures of the lending and ASC Library.

WHO MAY USE INTERLIBRARY LOAN

Students, staff members and faculty of Adams State College are
eligible for borrowing privileges from Interlibrary Loan Services
at Adams State College. Community patrons will be served if
their public library cannot meet their needs. Requests must be
submitted via a completed ILL request form.

Any library may request materials from our library. The request
must come on an OCLC or ALA form, or electronic mail. Libraries
will lose this privilege only if they are violators of the
National and/or Colorado Interlibrary Loan Codes.

TYPES OF MATERIALS AVAILABLE

The lending library determines what materials are or are not to
be loaned out. Generally reference materials, periodicals, rare
books, genealogical materials, videos, and bulky or fragile items
are not available. In some cases libraries do not lend
microfilm/microfiche materials, dissertations, thesis or any
other item not in their main collection.

Adams State College Library attempts to maintain as generous a
lending policy as possible. Any book in our main collection may
go out. Microfilm and microfiche requests will be handled by the
ILL Secretary or ILL Supervisor on a case by case basis. Films
and other A-V materials such as videos, computer software,
materials housed in the Colorado Room, Archives, or Reference are
not loaned out.

Adams State College Library
Alamosa, Colorado

MATERIALS REQUESTED OF OUR LIBRARY

Adams State College Library treats ILL patrons from other
libraries in the same manner as they would their own patrons.
Requested materials are checked out for 4 weeks and may be
renewed for three more weeks if no one has placed a hold on the
item. We reserve the right to recall the item however at any
time.

We will accept ILL requests via ALA Form, OCLC, electronic mail,
or Telefax. We will accept telephone requests under special
circumstances.

There are no ILL charges for books. There are also no charges
for photocopied materials up to the first thirty pages. If the
request is more than that amount we may charge $.10 per page for
all copies beyond thirty pages. The ILL Supervisor will make a
determination on any charges.

Adams State College ILL policies on charges, loan periods, etc.
are available to potential borrowers via the OCLC NAME-ADDRESS
Directory. They are subject to change at any time.

As per standard practice, and in accordance with national
guidelines, the borrowing library is responsible for replacing
any lost item. This is true if the loss occurs through patron
negligence or due to losses in the mail.

CHARGES AND THE USE OF INTERLIBRARY LOAN MATERIALS

Every effort will be made to locate lending libraries who do not charge for the use of their books and do not charge, or charge a minimal amount, for providing photocopies of periodical articles. If however the lending library does charge, and the patron has agreed to pay these charges, the ILL item will not be released until these monies are collected. If the patron refuses to pay, registration or graduation holds will be initiated.

The lending library has every right to place restrictions on the use of the borrowed item. A common restriction is "in-house" library use of valuable or irreplaceable items. The lending library determines due dates and these dates should be respected. Repeated disregard of this rule by any patron will lead to a revocation of ILL services to that patron until all materials have been returned or paid for. Any loss of borrowed materials will result in a charge to the patron. The replacement expense will be determined by the lending library and will be passed on to the borrowing patron.

TIME TO PROCESS

It is our goal to process our patrons requests and those from other libraries within 2-3 days.

RETURNING MATERIALS - AND RENEWAL REQUESTS

All materials borrowed should be returned to the ILL office when it is open. If this office is closed the materials should be left at the circulation desk. The patron should leave the ILL identification paper band on the book.

If a renewal is necessary the patron should notify the ILL office prior to the renewal date. Renewals are totally at the discretion of the lending library.

REPEATED DISREGARD OF LENDING LIBRARY DUE DATES BY ASC PATRONS, WILL RESULT IN THE LOSS OF ILL PRIVILEGES UNTIL ALL MATERIALS HAVE BEEN RETURNED OR PAID FOR.

Charles B. Phillips Library
Aurora University
Aurora, Illinois

AURORA UNIVERSITY INTERLIBRARY LOAN POLICY

"Each library has a responsibility to make every effort
to meet the reading needs of its community. Given the
wide range of user needs, this responsibility cannot be
met solely by its local collection. Therefore lending
materials among libraries for the use of individuals in
Illinois is vital to the public interest..."

Preface to the Illinois Interlibrary Loan Code 1988

A. DEFINITION

The Interlibrary Loan department of the Aurora University
Library provides a service through which its patrons can
obtain materials not currently available in the Aurora
University Library. The conditions of this service are based
on the American Library Association National Interlibrary
Loan Code, 1980, the Illinois Interlibrary Loan Code, 1988,
and by regulations of the individual lending libraries.

B. USERS OF INTERLIBRARY LOAN

Interlibrary Loan service is offered to all Aurora University
students, faculty, and staff. Patrons not currently
affiliated with the University are not eligible (i.e.
courtesy card patrons, high school students, alumni).

C. MATERIALS ELIGIBLE FOR INTERLIBRARY LOAN

Materials available for circulation to Aurora University
students are eligible for loan.

D. MATERIALS NOT AVAILABLE FOR INTERLIBRARY LOAN

a. Reference materials

b. Reserve materials

c. Periodicals (photocopies are provided instead)

d. Microforms (photocopies are provided instead)

e. Audiovisual materials by special arrangement only

f. Rare or valuable materials, including manuscripts

g. Bulky or fragile materials which are difficult or
   expensive to ship

. CHARGES

    a.   Books

        1.   There is no charge for monographs (books) loaned by Illinois libraries to Aurora University patrons.

        2.   Postage, insurance, and service charges are occasionally placed on monographs (books) loaned by libraries outside of Illinois; patron approval of these charges is required before the interlibrary loan transaction can be completed.

        3.   Fines may be charged for overdue materials.

        4.   Aurora University Library will charge $45 in the event an item from its collection is lost. Other libraries will have their own charges for lost items from their collections.

    b.   Periodical Articles

        1.   There will be a 10 cent charge per page for photocopies ordered by Aurora University patrons.

        2.   Special charges will be assessed if the patron requests special delivery services such as Express Mail, Federal Express, UPS, Fax, etc.

. DURATION

The time allowed for the loan is usually two to three weeks and is indicated on a yellow slip inserted in the borrowed item. Renewal of borrowed items should be requested prior to the due date for the same loan period originally granted. However, all borrowed materials are subject to recall and must be returned promptly.

. PROCEDURES

    a.   An interlibrary loan request form must be completed for each item requested. Forms are located at several places in the library (e.g. next to the LCS terminal in lobby and at the circulation and reference desks.)

    b.   It is recommended that a minimum of 14 days be allowed to fill the request.

    c.   Incomplete requests or requests for items already in our collection will be returned to the requestor.

    d.   Up to five (5) requests may be submitted on any one day.

> e. Requests may be left with the Interlibrary Loan Assistant or another senior staff member.
>
> f. Patrons are responsible for checking to see if their items have been received.
>
> g. Return books to the Circulation Desk.

H. PAYMENT FOR LOST ITEMS

> If a patron loses an item, s/he will be billed by the lending institution or the Aurora University Library for the item.

I. VIOLATIONS

> Should a patron repeatedly disregard the ILL guidelines, his/her ILL privileges will be withdrawn. Some actions which may result in suspension of privileges are: returning books late, not picking up requested material, and not paying for requested items (when appropriate).

J. RESPONSIBILITIES OF AURORA UNIVERSITY LIBRARY AS A LENDING LIBRARY

> a. Aurora University Library shall implement lending policies with due consideration for the needs of its primary clientele.
>
> b. Copies of this interlibrary loan policy statement shall be available upon request.
>
> c. Aurora University Library shall initiate processing of requests within one working day of receipt and shall complete the processing transaction within three working days of receipt.
>
> d. Aurora University Library shall notify the borrowing library promptly if materials are not being sent.
>
> e. Photocopy services and on-site use of non circulating collections are available.

K. RESPONSIBILITIES OF AURORA UNIVERSITY LIBRARY AS A BORROWING LIBRARY

> a. Aurora University Library is responsible for compliance with the copyright law (Title 17, U.S. Code) and its accompanying guidelines, and shall inform its users of the applicable portions of the law. An indication of compliance shall be provided with all copy requests.

b.   Aurora University Library shall use its local resources
     before initiating interlibrary loan requests.

c.   Materials requested shall be described as completely and
     accurately as possible, following accepted bibliographic
     practice. Verification shall utilize standard
     bibliographic tools and source verification shall be
     cited. When items cannot be verified, "cannot verify"
     shall be indicated on the request.

d.   If verification is disregarded, or if the bibliographic
     data is incorrect, the lending library may return the
     request unfilled without special effort to identify the
     reference.

e.   Aurora University Library shall honor the lending
     library's conditions of loan.

f.   While no acknowledgment of receipt is necessary, if
     there is undue delay in receipt of shipments, Aurora
     University Library shall notify the lending library.

g.   Unless specifically forbidden by the lending library,
     Aurora University Library patrons may copy any item
     provided that such copying is in accordance with the
     copyright law and no damage to the original material
     will result.

h.   Aurora University Library is responsible for: returning
     loans promptly; safety of materials; and all costs of
     repair or replacement in accordance with the policy of
     the lending library.

/89

College of Saint Mary Library
Interlibrary Loan Policy

I.   Definition

An interlibrary loan is a transaction in which library
material, or a copy of the material, is made available by a
library to another upon request.

II.   Purpose

The purpose of interlibrary loan is to obtain library
material not available in the College of Saint Mary Library
and to loan material found in the College of Saint Mary
Library which is not available in other libraries.

III.   Conditions of service

The conditions of this service are set by the National
Interlibrary Loan Code, 1980; special interlibrary
loan agreements with consortia such as PICKLE and ICON; and
laws, rules, and procedures pertaining to interlibrary loan
activity promulgated by the State of Nebraska.

IV.   Interlibrary Borrowing

    A.   This service is offered to students, faculty, and
        staff of College of Saint Mary.

    B.   Material which may be borrowed.

           1.   A loan or a copy of any material may be
               requested from another library although
               the lending library will decide in each
               case whether or not a particular item can
               be provided. Items missing from the
               College of Saint Mary Library's collection
               may be borrowed. Photocopy of missing
               pages from library material can be
               obtained.

           2.   Most libraries will not ordinarily lend
               the following types of material:

               Rare or valuable material, including
               manuscripts;
               Bulky or fragile items that are difficult or
               expensive to ship;
               Material in high demand at the lending
               library;
               Material with local circulation
               restrictions:
               Unique material that would be difficult or
               impossible to replace.

3.   Materials which will not be borrowed include:

Books owned by the College of Saint Mary
Library and temporarily in use;
Materials for class, reserve, or other group
use;

C.   Borrower's responsibilities.

1.   An interlibrary borrowing request must be
submitted in writing on appropriate forms with
complete bibliographic information.

2.   The source of where the information was found
must be included.

3.   There must be an indication of compliance with
the Copyright Law (Title 17, U.S. Code) where
required.

4.   There is a 50 cent non-refundable processing
fee payable at the time the interlibrary loan
request is made. Payment must be made for
charges by the lending library.

D.   Service will be given as speedily and inexpensively
as conditions permit. Usually material may be
obtained within 10 days.

E.   Statistics will be kept in accordance with internal,
State, and Federal guidelines and requirements.

V.   Interlibrary Lending.

A.   This service is offered to other publicly supported
or not-for-profit libraries which abide by the
conditions set forth in the National Interlibrary
Loan code and agreements with PICKLE and ICON.

B.   Materials which ordinarily circulate to College of
Saint Mary Library users may be sent out on
interlibrary loan. This does not include
periodicals, reference materials, microfilm,
microfiche, or audio-visual materials.

C.   Borrowing library's responsibilities.

1.   The borrowing library must submit requests in
standard format as prescribed by the documents
and agreements described in III. above. The
College of Saint Mary will accept requests by
ALA forms, OCLC, telephone, fax, or electronic
mail.

        2. Books are on loan for 28 days. Photocopies not have to be returned. College of Saint Mary Library does not charge other librarie for interlibrary loan.

    D. Service will be given as speedily as conditions permit. A 3-day turnaround time for requests fro College of Saint Mary is the goal.

Interlibrary Loan Policy Concordia University

Outline
Interlibrary Loan Policy
    I. Statement of the Library's Mission
    II. Mission of the ILL Department
    III. Purpose of ILL Guidelines
    IV. ILL Staff
    V. ILL Users and Services
    VI. Charges for ILL
        A. Borrowing
        B. Lending
Interlibrary Loan Procedures
    VIII. Books
        A. Initiating requests
        B. Filling requests
    IX. Photocopy
        A. Initiating requests
        B. Filling requests
    X. ERIC documents
    XI. Statistics

I. Statement of the Library's Mission

The mission of library services of Concordia University is to acquire and organize print and audiovisual resources needed for the support of the current and anticipated instructional research and service activities of the University; to assist the users in efficiently accessing and utilizing these resources and non-Concordia resources for their information and educational needs; and to provide the media facilities and services required to support the educational, research and general needs of the University community.

II. Mission of the ILL Department

It is the mission of the ILL department to locate and acquire, whenever possible, materials not owned by Concordia for the educational, research, and general needs of the University community. This may include, but is not limited to, books, journal articles, documents, and audio-visual materials. The ILL department is also responsible for the lending of materials owned by Concordia to other institutions when the requests fall into the guidelines stated here.

Concordia's ILL department complies with ALA guidelines, the Illinois Interlibrary Loan Code July 1988, the copyright law (Title 17, US Code), and the LIBRAS Interlibrary Loan policy.

III. Purpose of ILL Guidelines

The purpose of this statement is to describe the services and resources which are offered by the department, to set standards and guidelines for service, to provide guidance for those working in the ILL department and those being trained and to serve as a source of policy information for potential borrowing institutions.

IV. ILL Staff

ILL staff serve as the link between the Concordia library and other institutions. Each staff member should be familiar with the bibiliographic tools available, i.e., OCLC, IO, SLS/LIBRAS Union List of Serials, etc. ILL staff should also be aware of and make use of services available through the Suburban Library System, LIBRAS, ILCSO and other consortia.

V. ILL Users and Services

The library provides ILL services to all Concordia students, faculty and staff. Non-Concordia students and SLS patrons will be directed to their local institution for initiating ILL requests.

Patrons wishing to initiate an ILL must fill out an ILL form, available at the main level desk. When materials are available from Rosary College or from the Oak Park or River Forest Public Libraries, the patron will be asked to go directly to these libraries for materials.

The library loans out items from the general collection, the juvenille collection and ERIC documents. Non-circulating collections include the reference collection, audio-visual materials, periodicals, and the curriculum library.

The library also provides photocopies from journals and fiche copies of ERIC documents. Concordia does not provide paper copies of ERIC documents.

It is the responsibility of the Head of ILL to make sure that no more than five articles are requested from any one journal title.

VI. Charges for ILL
A. Borrowing

Except where there is a charge by the lending institution, ILL services are provided at no cost to the patron. When there is a charge by the lending institution, every effort will be made to contact the patron before initiating a request.

B. Lending

Concordia lends materials to Illinois libraries for free. There is a $6.00 fee for out-of-state requests.

VII. Methods of delivery

Concordia accepts ILL requests through FAX, U.S. Mail, or ILDS. ERIC document requests may be received over the telephone.

Articles of 10 pages or less will be FAXed to the requesting institution, unless otherwise stated.

Items sent to libraries in Illinois will be sent through the Inter-library delivery system. Items sent out of Illinois will be sent through U.S. Mail.

No books or magazine articles will be sent through the Chicago

Library System.

NOTE: The second half of this document serves as the official procedures for initiating and filling ILL requests. The breakdown is as follows.
> VIII. Books
>> A. Initiating requests
>> B. Filling requests
> IX. Photocopy
>> A. Initiating requests
>> B. Filling requests
> X. ERIC documents
> XI. Statistics

VIII. Books
A. Initiating requests

Any patron wishing to initiate an ILL request must fill out an ILL form, available at the main level desk. Information should be legible and as complete as possible.

Requests should be given to the reference librarian on duty. The librarian will search Illinet Online and OCLC for holders of the item. The librarian may either print out a list of potential lenders, or note them at the bottom of the form.

The form will then be given to the ILL clerk who will send the request to the potential lenders in the following order of preference: LIBRAS, ILLINET, OCLC, and SLS.

The ILL clerk will notify the patron of any potential charges for borrowing the item.

When the item arrives, the ILL clerk will call the patron, informing them that the item has arrived. The patron's name and the due date will be noted on the book and the book will be placed on the will call shelf.

When the item is returned to Concordia, it will be promptly returned to the lending institution in the same manner that it was sent.

B. Filling requests

Requests may be received via mail, Fax, ILDS or OCLC. If the request is coming from out-of-state, it will be determined if the borrowing library is willing to pay a $6.00 out-of-state fee. If not, the request is returned indicating that it will not be filled.

Requests coming from LIBRAS libraries, SLS libraries or other Illinois libraries will be filled at no charge to the borrowing institution.

Due date for books is three weeks from the current date. One copy of the request with the due date should be kept for each item loaned out.

Books sent to Illinois libraries will be sent ILDS, except when the item is going to a member of the Chicago Library System, then the item will be sent through the mail at library rate. Any books going out of Illinois will be sent through the mail at library rate.

The circulation card for each book is pulled and the due date and the borrowing library are noted on the circulation card.

Appropriate forms for SLS, LIBRAS and OCLC requests should be filled out.

IX. Photocopy
A. Initiating requests

Any patron wishing to initiate an ILL request must fill out an ILL request form, available at the front desk. Information should be legible and as complete as possible. The ILL department reserves the right to return any ILL request that is lacking verification information.

The student or librarian receiving the request will note their initials on one corner and give it to the Head of ILL. The Head of ILL will use the resources available to locate potential owners of the item. (SLS/LIBRAS Union List of Serials, NSLS Union List of Serials, SILO, OCLC) Requests will be sent to potential owners in the following order of preference: LIBRAS, SLS and OCLC.

The Head of ILL will notify the patron of any potential charges before initiating the request.

When the item arrives, the patron's name will be put on the item and the item will be placed in the appropriate hanging file on the will call shelf at the main level desk. The Head of ILL will notify the patron that their materials have arrived.

The Head of ILL will make sure that no more than five articles per year are requested from any one journal.

B. Filling requests

Requests may be received via mail, Fax, ILDS or OCLC. If the request is coming from out-of-state, it will be determined if the borrowing library is willing to pay a $6.00 out-of-state fee, plus $.10 per page for articles longer than 10 pages. If not, the request is returned indicating that it will not be filled.

Requests coming from LIBRAS libraries, SLS libraries or other Illinois libraries will be filled at no charge to the borrowing institution.

There are no due dates for photocopies sent.

Articles of 10 pages or less will be FAXed to the requesting institution. Articles of 10 pages or more will be sent to Illinois libraries ILDS except where the article is being sent to a library within the Chicago Library System, in which case the item will be sent through U.S. Mail. Out of state requests will be sent through U.S. Mail.

One copy of each request should be kept for each photocopy supplied for the current year.

When the request comes from the SLS Photocopy service, the article will be sent directly to the borrowing institution and one copy of the request indicating shipment will be sent to the SLS Photocopy service.

X. ERIC documents

Requests for ERIC documents may arrive via mail, FAX, or ILDS or may be taken over the phone.

ERIC documents may be borrowed by Suburban Library System members. Loans are for three weeks.

ERIC documents are copied from fiche to fiche. Concordia does

not make paper copies of ERIC documents.
    Charges for duplication are $.10 per fiche for LIBRAS
libraries, $.25 per fiche for all other institutions. A bill will
be sent with the fiche.
    Individual institutions may wish to set up different methods
of payment for this service.

XI. Statistics

    The following statistics need to be kept by the ILL department
on a monthly basis.
    ERIC fiche loaned
    ERIC fiche - duplicates sent
    Books loaned - LIBRAS
    Books loaned - SLS
    Books loaned - OCLC
    Books loaned - ALA, other
    Books borrowed - LIBRAS
    Books borrowed - SLS
    Books borrowed - OCLC
    Books borrowed - ALA, other
    Photocopies sent - LIBRAS
    Photocopies sent - SLS
    Photocopies sent - Other
    Photocopies received - LIBRAS
    Photocopies received - SLS
    Photocopies received - Other

March 23, 1992

FORT VALLEY STATE COLLEGE LIBRARY
INTERLIBRARY LOAN POLICIES

Interlibrary loan encompasses both borrowing and lending, both the sending of materials and the providing of reproductions. In essence, the purpose of interlibrary loan is to borrow or obtain copies of library materials not found in a library's collection on behalf of the library's patrons and to lend or provide copies of library materials requested by other libraries.

Interlibrary loan policies are best organized in two parts.

1. Incoming (lending) activities, involving requests from other libraries for access to materials, at Fort Valley State College.

2. Outgoing (borrowing) activities, involving requests from the borrowing library's patrons for materials which are not owned by the library.

INCOMING LENDING POLICIES:

1. THE INTERLIBRARY LOAN PERSONNEL WILL MAKE JUDGEMENT ABOUT THE ELIGIBILITY OF BORROWING LIBRARIES. The library will supply widely owned materials requested by academic and public libraries.

2. THE INTERLIBRARY LOAN PERSONNEL WILL MAKE JUDGEMENT ABOUT THE ELIGIBILITY OF THE BORROWING LIBRARY'S PATRON. Requests for undergraduates will be refused. The major effort in an interlibrary loan transaction is generally undertaken by the borrowing library.

3. THE INTERLIBRARY LOAN PERSONNEL WILL MAKE JUDGEMENT ABOUT LENDING MATERIALS. Books which circulate in-house but seem inappropriate for interlibrary loan will not be shipped if the cost of shipping the material exceeds the amount of the material(i.e. paperback novels).

4. INTERLIBRARY LOAN MATERIALS NOT CIRCULATED AT FORT VALLEY STATE COLLEGE WILL BE LOANED TO OTHER LIBRARIES. Materials not circulated at Fort Valley State College will be loaned if the material is for research or if the material can be photocopied.

5. ATTEMPTS TO UNRAVEL IMPROPERLY PRESENTED REQUESTS WILL BE SEARCHED. The lending library will search for improper requests by deciphering abbreviated titles, searching for unverified citations and by a telephone call to the borrowing library.

6. PHOTOCOPY REQUESTS WHICH ARE BELIEVED TO BE IN VIOLATION OF THE COPYRIGHT LAW WILL BE DENIED AND RETURNED TO THE BORROWING LIBRARY.

7. BOOKS ON LOAN TO FORT VALLEY STATE COLLEGE PATRONS WILL BE RECALLED FOR INTERLIBRARY REQUESTS. Providing that the patron has used the book for the specified two weeks and not in need of the book for an additional period of time, this material will be shipped to the borrowing library.

8. ALL MATERIALS LOANED TO OTHER LIBRARIES WILL BE SHIPPED. Books and photocopies will be shipped by library rate; media sources and rare materials will be insured. All mailing will be handled via Post Office.

9. THERE IS NO CHARGE FOR PHOTOCOPYING SERVICES FROM SOME LIBRARIES. Provided that the number of pages to be copied does not exceed 20 pages.

OUTGOING (BORROWING) POLICIES

1. THERE ARE THREE DIFFERENT FORMS FOR REQUEST OF MATERIALS. Patrons are advised to be specific in requesting the type of form needed: (1) books (2) photocopy (3) dissertations, pamphlets and thesis.

2. FORT VALLEY STATE COLLEGE WILL NOT BORROW FOR UNDERGRADUATES. Administration, Faculty, Staff and Graduates currently employed or enrolled will be permitted to use the Interlibrary Loan Service.

3. TRANSACTIONS OF ANY SORT WILL BE REQUESTED BY THE OTHER LIBRARIES. Funds for postage or photocopying service will be determined by the lending library.

4. COPYRIGHT GUIDELINES ARE PRINTED ON THE FORM FOR PHOTOCOPY REQUESTED. Any request found to be in violation of the copyright law will be denied.

5. MATERIALS WILL BE BORROWED FROM LENDING LIBRARIES IN-STATE AND OUT-OF-STATE. The selection in choosing how materials will be ordered is determined by which lending library is the closest and does not charge.

6. THERE IS NO CHARGE FOR ANY REQUESTS IN-COMING OR OUT-GOING.

7. RENEWALS ARE GRANTED TO BORROWING LIBRARIES PROVIDED THAT FORT VALLEY STATE COLLEGE PATRONS ARE NOT IN NEED OF THAT MATERIAL.

8. PATRONS WHO HAVE BEHAVED IRRESPONSIBLY(not returned materials or not paid fines from lending libraries) WILL BE REFUSED INTERLIBRARY LOAN SERVICES.

9. THE LENGTH OF TIME TO RETRIEVE MATERIALS THROUGH INTERLIBRARY LOAN IS USUALLY TWO WEEKS, depending on the lending library availibity to loan the material.

10. THE LENDING LIBRARY WILL DETERMINE ALL COSTS OF MATERIALS SUPPLIED TO BORROWING LIBRARY, IF ANY.

11. THE PATRON WILL BE NOTIFIED BY TELEPHONE WHEN INTERLIBRARY LOAN MATERIAL ARRIVES.

12. THE PATRON SHOULD GIVE A COMPLETE AND ACCURATE CITATION TO ENSURE THAT THE CORRECT ITEM IS BEING ORDERED.

13. THE DATE DUE FOR BOOKS WILL BE STAMPED ON THE DATE DUE PLATE OF THE LENDING LIBRARY.

14. INTERLIBRARY LOAN IS NOT A RIGHT, BUT A PRIVILEGE AND THERE IS NO GUARANTEE THAT, IF A REQUEST IS SENT, THE MATERIAL WILL BE LOANED.

INTERLIBRARY LOAN POLICY

Ryan Library
Point Loma Nazarene College

The Reference Department assumes the responsibility of providing interlibrary loan service to the PLNC community and in filling requests from outside borrowing institutions (or individuals). The National Interlibrary Loan Code and the METRO Interlibrary Loan Code are followed.

ILL and Copyright:

Patrons requesting an interlibrary loan, sign the request form indicating that they have read the copyright warning and take responsibility for any photocopies received. Records are kept of all photocopies requested and received for three years in compliance with CONTU Guidelines for the Proviso of Subsection 108 (g)(2).

Borrowing Guidelines:

In accordance with the National Interlibrary Loan Code, "Requests for individuals with academic affiliations should be limited to those materials needed for faculty and staff research, and the thesis and dissertation research of graduate students."[1] As a member of the San Diego Greater Metropolitan Area Library Council (METRO), lending among libraries for the use of an individual has been encouraged as it is in the public interest.[2] This means that after exhausting the resources in Ryan and Rohr Libraries, materials may be requested on interlibrary loan by any individual. Local library resources (San Diego Public Library, San Diego State University, University of San Diego, etc.) are checked first. If materials are not available locally, the search is automatically expanded for faculty and graduate students. The librarian's discretion is to be used in expanding searches beyond the local area for undergraduates or other users.

As a borrowing library, every attempt possible is made to verify each request and locate holding libraries before sending out the request. Materials which are available in print at a reasonable price are not requested on interlibrary loan.

Lending Guidelines:

Requests for materials housed in Ryan Library's circulating collection are loaned for one month unless the librarian determines that the material is in demand by campus users. Materials recently cataloged must be available for in-house use six months before lending on interlibrary loan. Other items which do not circulate are: reference books, periodicals, curriculum guides, textbooks, and archival materials. Requests for photocopy must indicate compliance with copyright guidelines.

---

[1] Sarah Katherine Thomson. _Interlibrary Loan Procedure Manual_. (Chicago: American Library Association, 1970), p.2.

[2] _METRO Directory_. "METRO Interlibrary Loan Code - Appendix E." (San Diego, CA: San Diego Greater Metropolitan Area Library Council), p.291.

INTERLIBRARY LOAN POLICY

Southwest Baptist University

I. Introduction

Interlibrary loan is a service provided to obtain materials which are not available in the university library. Conditions of this service are governed by the National Interlibrary Loan Code (adopted by the American Library Association), the Copyright Law, Title 17, U.S. Code (see Library Policy on Copyright), and the Southwest Baptist University Interlibrary Loan Policy.

Some materials which cannot be borrowed are periodicals (other than photocopies), audio-visual materials, reference books, rare books, or materials found in special collections. Books owned by this library and temporarily in use may not be borrowed.

II. Borrowing

To request an interlibrary loan, the library user must fill out the proper interlibrary loan form recording all information necessary for the locating of the material to be borrowed or photocopied. Signing the interlibrary loan form indicates the user has been made aware of copyright violations and limitations and costs which may be incurred.

A. Time

The time needed to obtain an interlibrary loan is dependent upon the difficulty of the request, proximity of the lending library, and the amount of requests to be processed. A minimum of seven (7) to ten (10) days is needed to search, process, and receive each request.

B. Charges

Because interlibrary loan is considered a service for the students, faculty and staff of SBU, no service charge is assessed for locating and requesting materials for academic use. However, borrowers are responsible for any fees, such as photocopy charges, postage reimbursement, or handling fees, imposed by the lending institution even if material is no longer needed upon arrival.

Interlibrary loans not picked up two weeks after arrival will be charged to the borrower with a $2.00 per item processing fee.

Fax services are available for periodical article requests. Charges will be $.10 per page in addition to charges assessed by the lending library (see Library Telefacsimile Policy).

Any charges due must be paid upon receipt of the material. Faculty may have costs charged to their departmental budget.

C. Free Periodical Articles

In some cases a student may be eligible to receive a periodical article free except for a $.10 per page photocopy cost (see Policy on Provision of Periodical Articles).

D. <u>Non-university Personnel</u>

A non-refundable $2.00 service charge will be assessed to pay computer cost for searching and requesting of material. In addition, any fees assessed by the lending institution are also the responsibility of the non-university person.

E. <u>Notification</u>

Borrower will be notified when material arrives. Material must be picked up within two weeks.

F. <u>Loan Period</u>

The lending library determines the length of loan and restrictions concerning where the material may be used. Some items may be restricted to "in library use only". Renewals may or may not be granted depending upon the policy of the lending library.

G. <u>Overdue Material</u>

Materials, other than photocopies, must be returned on or before the due date. Overdue or lost materials will be subject to the same fines and policies as those overdue from the university library (see Library Policy Regarding Lost, Damaged or Overdue Library Materials and Fines or Charges). In the case of the lending library imposing a fine, that charge must be paid by the borrower.

III. <u>Lending</u>

Southwest Baptist University will honor requests received through (1) OCLC, (2) ALA form if borrowing library is not an OCLC participant, or (3) University Interlibrary Loan forms to be used by off-campus sites and area schools.

The university interlibrary loan policy is available to libraries via the OCLC Name address directory, the Missouri Union List of Serials and Periodicals Directory or upon request.

A. <u>Materials not Loaned</u>

1. Reference books
2. Periodicals (photocopies of articles will be furnished)
3. Reserve materials
4. Vertical file materials
5. Southern Baptist Convention materials
6. Missouri documents
7. Archival materials
8. Audio-visual materials
9. High demand materials

B. <u>Copyright Compliance</u>

All interlibrary loan functions shall be directed by and in compliance with the Copyright Law and its guidelines. In order to accomplish this compliance, the library will adhere to the copyright guidelines in regard to CCG and CCL.

The requesting library shall indicate compliance with CCG or CCL (see Guidelines for Photocopying for Interlibrary Loans section of the Southwest Baptist University Library Policy on Copyright).

In addition, the library will:

1.   Treat all requests from Southwest Baptist University College
      centers as orders from the Library.

2.   Reserve the right to turn down any interlibrary loan request
      if, in our opinion, it violates the Copyright Law and its
      guidelines.

C.   Charges

No general handling charge will be assessed. Photocopy charges are
$.10 per page and fax charges are $.50 per page.

OCLC participating libraries submitting ALA request forms will be
charged a $2.00 service fee.

D.   Loan Period

Materials, except photocopies, are loaned for one (1) month.
Depending upon condition and format, some items may be restricted to
"in library use only".

Renewals are granted for two weeks if the item is not in demand.

E.   Overdues

When an item has been overdue two (2) weeks, it will be recalled
and/or a note requesting status will be sent.

When an item has been overdue one (1) month, a bill will be sent to
the borrowing library requesting payment.   Payment will be
determined according to the Library Policy Regarding Lost, Damaged
or Overdue Library Materials and Fines or Charges.

LENDING POLICY FACT SHEETS

AURORA UNIVERSITY LIBRARY

INTERLIBRARY LOAN POLICY

FACT SHEET

Aurora University Library agrees to make its materials available
to other libraries. Our library will decide whether a particular
item should or should not be provided, and whether the original or
a copy should be sent. The conditions of this service are based
on the American Library Association National Interlibrary Loan
Code, 1980, and the Illinois Interlibrary Loan Code, 1988.

Address for Interlibrary Loan:

Aurora University Library
Interlibrary Loan Department
347 South Gladstone
Aurora, IL 60506

Phone: (312)844-5437
Fax: (312)892-9286

OCLC Code: ICA
LCS Code: AR

Books:

Will lend those that circulate.
Loan period:
3 weeks in Illinois
4 weeks out of state
Renewals may be requested

Periodicals:
Will not lend.
Photocopy service available.

Newspapers:
Will not lend.
Photocopy service available.

Microforms:
Will not lend.
Photocopy service available.

Audio-Visual Materials: Will not lend.

Dissertations: Will lend circulating copies

Charges: No charges for Illinois borrowers. Invoices for postage
and handling and photocopy charges of 10 cents per page will
accompany materials sent to out-of-state borrowers.

Remarks: Requests may be made through OCLC, IO, Fax, or ALA form.
Each request must be verified and the verification source
noted. When items cannot be verified, "cannot verify" shall
be indicated on the request. Material recalled for an Aurora
University patron must be returned promptly regardless of due
date.

KENDRICK LIBRARY
EVANGEL COLLEGE
INTERLIBRARY LOAN POLICY

INTERLIBRARY LOAN OFFICE:

Barb Willard
Interlibrary Loans
Kendrick Library
Evangel College
1111 N. Glenstone Ave.
Springfield, MO 65802

TELEPHONE:
Voice: (417) 865-2815 Ext. 7323
Facsimile: (417) 865-1574

OFFICE HOURS:
M-F 8:00 TO 4:30

CODES:
NUC Code: MoSpE
OCLC Code: MOE

FORMS ACCEPTED:
OCLC
ALA
FAX

BOOKS:
Length of loan: 30 Days
Renew: Once - 20 Days
Charges: Usually none

PHOTOCOPY SERVICE:
25 cents per page
$3.00 Minimum
Handling charge: Included

MICROFORMS:
25 cents per page
$3.00 Minimum
Handling charge: Included
(May lend under unusual
circumstances.)

THESES & DISSERTATIONS:
Lend under special circumstances.

BILLING POLICY:
Invoiced with material

FACSIMILE:
Charge per page:
Interstate:
25 cents per page
$3.00 Minimum
In MO, AK, HI and Canada:
50 cents per page
$3.00 Minumum
International:
$4.00 first page
$2.00 per additional page
Telephone charge: Included

NON-CIRCULATING:
Reference
Audio-visual
Microforms
Newspapers
Periodicals
Children's Literature
Curriculum Lab materials
Popular & Recreational fiction
Devotional & Inspirational
Reserve

AFFILIATIONS:
OCLC
MLNC
SWMLN Group Access
CL@N Group Access
MIGI Group Access
SWMALC Agreement

REMARKS:

1. LOST MATERIALS will be invoiced at current market value plus $10.00 p/c. DAMAGES will be billed at cost.

2. Consideration to loaning NON-CIRCULATING materials will be made on a case-by-case basis. Please telephone before requesting.

3. ADDITIONAL $5.00 CHARGE for handling mail forms from full OCLC libraries.

Rev 10/10/1991

SIMPSON COLLEGE

LIBRARY

INTERLIBRARY LOAN POLICIES, 1992
OCLC Code: IOK

oks: Will lend all except Special Collections. Loan period: 4 weeks. Loans
may be renewed, usually for 2 weeks. Reference books are loaned at our
discretion.

riodicals: Generally not loaned.

croforms: Loaned at our discretion. Microform periodicals are usually not loaned.

Materials: Videos, LP's, films, CD's filmstrips/loops are not loaned. Cassette
recordings usually will be loaned.

will accept interlibrary loan requests via **OCLC, ICAN** (during the academic year only),
FAX, ALA form, and telephone. Our FAX number is (515) 961-1363. The Interlibrary
Loan Office phone number is (515) 961-1520.

nn Library participates in the **BCR/AMIGOS ILL Code**, the **IPAL** network, various local
agreements, and the **Iowa Courier Program.** We also are in the State Library of
Iowa's **Net Lender Reimbursement** program. Dunn Library is a member of the
Copyright Clearance Center. Our collection is nearly 100% in machine-readable
format, and holdings appear in OCLC. The periodical collection is fully listed
in the **Iowa Union List of Serials.**

nn Library does not charge for interlibrary loan service. We FAX articles upon request. However, since the **Iowa Courier Program** generally offers overnight delivery, we will use it for articles whenever possible, and would appreciate same.
Our materials may be shipped in Jiffy Bags unless we request otherwise.

nn Library participates in Iowa's **Open Access Program.** Thus, any Iowa resident with
a valid public library card is free to check out our materials, and anyone may
use our facility. However, we request that our community borrowers contact
their public library for interlibrary loan service.

rther questions? Contact Patricia Mayhew or Mike Wright at the above number.

508 North C Street   Indianola, Iowa 50125   515-961-1663

BORROWING POLICIES/
SERVICE BROCHURES

INTERLIBRARY LOAN
BORROWING POLICIES AND GUIDELINES (3/92)

Mikkelsen Library
Augustana College

I. PURPOSE

The purpose of interlibrary loan is to borrow or obtain
copies of library materials not found in our collection for
Augustana employees and students. This is accomplished
through a variety of computer networks and delivery systems.

The generally accepted philosophy of interlibrary loan is to
fill information needs by using cooperative arrangements
including local and regional consortia. To best meet
Augustana's information needs, Mikkelsen Library participates
in numerous resource sharing arrangements and networks.
Interlibrary loan serves as a supplemental source of
information, not as a substitute for developing our own local
collection.

II. COOPERATIVE AGREEMENTS

The National Interlibrary Loan Code, 1980, governs when and
how requests are made to other libraries within the United
States. Other local arrangements may further dictate
specific policies and procedures and, therefore, may take
precedence.

Mikkelsen Library works cooperatively with other libraries
within South Dakota in accordance with the South Dakota
Interlibrary Loan Code, 1979. Through the South Dakota State
Library (Pierre), we have a contract with the state of
Minnesota to use their collections. This service is
implemented by the MINITEX agency located at the University
of Minnesota. By virtue of our contract with Minnesota we
also have increased access to North Dakota libraries and
selected Wisconsin libraries.

III. CLIENTELE

Mikkelsen Library provides interlibrary loan service for
Augustana faculty, staff and currently enrolled students.
Graduate students who have asked for library privileges while
finishing theses may also make interlibrary loan requests.
Library Associates may use the ILL service for a $5.00
handling fee per request.

All other individuals (including alumni) are referred to
their "home" libraries for ILL services. In the case of

students, the home library is located at the institution
where they are enrolled. In the case of the general public,
the home library is their public library.

IV. INAPPROPRIATE REQUESTS

There are categories of materials which are generally
noncirculating and would not be available via interlibrary
loan:

--Rare or valuable material - examples would include anything
  published before 1800, manuscripts by famous people, items
  not generally available for purchase

--Large or fragile material - shipping may be difficult or
  cause damage

--High demand items - best sellers, newly published, current
  events, textbooks, reserve items

--Noncirculating items - reference books, periodicals
  (both whole issues and bound volumes), dissertations
  (except from degree granting institution, also available
  for purchase from UMI), audiovisual materials (high demand
  and expensive to replace), and sometimes genealogy (high
  demand)

--Technical reports - NTIS documents are readily available
  for purchase, other reports may be proprietary and not
  available for the public

V. COPYRIGHT CONSIDERATIONS

The borrowing library is responsible for conforming to
copyright law and guidelines. Mikkelsen Library abides by
the Copyright Act of 1976 and its subsequent interpretations
including the U.S. Copyright Office Circular R21,
<u>Reproduction of Copyrighted Works by Educators and Librarians</u>
and the National Commission on New Technological Uses of
Copyrighted Works (CONTU) guidelines on "Photocopying
Interlibrary Arrangements."

Generally, photocopying should not replace purchase of a
subscription or purchase of items in high demand. The
commonly accepted rule of thumb is no more than five articles
published within the last five years from any single journal
title. This guideline is applied to requests from the
library (not just the individual) on an annual basis.
Government documents are excluded from copyright limitations.

VI. MAKING A REQUEST

Patrons need to fill out one interlibrary loan request form
per item. Phone requests are taken at the discretion of the
staff. The interlibrary loan staff will find locations for
the material using a variety of tools including PALS, OCLC,
MULS, and other union lists. It is, however, helpful to know
where the patron got the information or citation. For
example, journal title abbreviations will vary depending on
which index or database is used.

VII. COSTS AND FINES

Most interlibrary loans are done at no charge. Exceptions
occur when we must go to libraries not included in our
cooperative agreements and when articles requested are
lengthy. Many libraries outside of our geographic region
charge a handling fee plus a per page charge. South Dakota
libraries charge only when the article exceeds 25 pages.

Staff will contact the requestor if charges will be assessed.
Patrons are asked on the form to indicate how much they would
be willing to pay as a method of saving time. Costs which
are incurred are passed along to the requesting patron.

Borrowed items which are overdue are subject to a fine of ten
cents per day up to a maximum of $2.00 per item. The fine
policy for ILL material is the same as the policy for our own
material.

VIII. TURNAROUND TIME

Requests are processed as quickly as possible. Library staff
use a variety of electronic systems to speed this process.
Material found within the state or at the University of
Minnesota are usually received within a week. Going further
afield requires more time for delivery. The patron's
deadline should take this into consideration.

IX. RUSH REQUESTS

Rush requests are done at the discretion of the library
staff. Library patrons are first encouraged to utilize the
local collection to its fullest. Fax delivery is possible at
a cost of $.25 per page (see fax policy for details).
Overnight courier service is available from several locations
at no additional cost. Charges incurred are passed along to
the requesting patron.

X. RENEWALS

Renewals are seldom allowed for interlibrary loan material.
Each lending library has its own renewal policy, so it is
necessary to contact the lending library to get renewal
permission. Because of the amount of time required to submit
a renewal request, receive a response and then contact the
patron, we encourage using the material as quickly as
possible.

INTERLIBRARY LOAN POLICY

GEISLER LEARNING RESOURCE CENTER
CENTRAL COLLEGE
PELLA, IOWA

INTERLIBRARY LOAN: AN INTRODUCTION

Interlibrary loan is a service through which library material (or a copy of the material) is made available by one library to another. The purpose of interlibrary loan is to obtain library material not available in the LRC. The LRC offers this service to students and faculty as a supplement to the library collection, and not as a substitute for it. Every effort should be made to exhaust LRC resources before utilizing Interlibrary Loan. To this end, faculty and librarians are encouraged to build the collection in their areas of expertise, with an eye to the forthcoming research needs of Central College students.

The LRC belongs to national, regional and local networks. Consequently, our Interlibrary Loan service must be in accord with our various contractual agreements and obligations, including the copyright laws. The LRC borrows and lends according to the National Interlibrary Code of 1980 and complies with the copyright law (Title 17, U.S. Code) and its accompanying guidelines. The LRC depends ultimately on the willingness of other libraries to lend to us. Of course, the LRC must in turn lend its own material to other libraries.

WHO MAY USE INTERLIBRARY LOAN?

CUI students, faculty, and professional staff. Public Patrons must use the services of their nearest Public Library.

WHAT CAN BE BORROWED ON INTERLIBRARY LOAN?

Books, photocopied articles, some microforms, and some government publications: all subject to copyright restrictions.

WHAT CANNOT BE BORROWED ON INTERLIBRARY LOAN?

Rare or valuable materials including manuscripts; bulky or fragile items which are difficult to ship; material in high demand at the lending library; unique materials which would be difficult to replace; Reference and non-circulating books; current issues or entire bound volumes of periodicals.

HOW TO USE INTERLIBRARY LOAN

Interlibrary Loan request forms are available only from a Librarian or from the Interlibrary Loan Assistant. The request forms must be completed in full, including the final date the

item can be used. Since Interlibrary Loan should be utilized
only after LRC resources have been exhausted, consultation with
the Reference Staff prior to submitting a request is required.
For periodical requests, the patron must provide full journal
title (no abbreviations) and source of reference.

ARE THERE CHARGES OR RESTRICTIONS ON INTERLIBRARY LOAN?

At present, this service is offered free of charge. However,
since the cost to the LRC in terms of staff time and system fees
is substantial and we try to serve all patrons equally, the
number of requests accepted from an individual at peak times may
be limited. Patrons are asked to rank requests numerically in
order of importance or preference.

HOW LONG WILL IT TAKE?

One should expect to wait up to three weeks for arrival of
material. Often the waiting period is less; however,
expectations should not be based on a shorter turn-around time.

WHAT ABOUT FAX?

Because of the expense to lending libraries and the unreliability
of telefacsimile transmission, photocopied materials are normally
received via U.S. mails. However, when librarians determine that
CUI students, faculty or staff involved in research have
legitimate time constraints, librarians will ask to have
photocopies FAXED to the college. Once again, users should not
expect to receive materials sooner than 3 to 5 days because our
requests are dependent on the lending library's willingness to
give "rush" service. (SEE ALSO LRC Interlibrary Loan FAX Policy)

USE OF BORROWED MATERIALS

In order to make Interlibrary Loan an effective service, it is
necessary to maintain good relations with cooperating libraries.
Loan periods and use restrictions are set by the lending library
and must be strictly complied with. Normally books and
microforms may be used for two weeks though times may vary.
Books must be picked up in person at the LRC and returned
promptly to either the Circulation or Interlibrary Loan Desks.
Photocopies are sent to LRC patrons via campus mail and may be
used as long as necessary.

LRC
3/13/84
Revised 7/89; 11/90; 11/91 rem

EMERSON
COLLEGE

Interlibrary Loan Policy

No library can fulfill all the needs of its community through its own holdings. Therefore, libraries supplement their holdings with Interlibrary Loans (ILLs), borrowing needed materials from other libraries. These transactions are governed by the National Interlibrary Loan Code, which is explained in the <u>Interlibrary Loan Procedure Manual</u>. "The purpose of interlibrary loan is to make available, for <u>research</u>, materials not owned by a given library.... It is assumed that each library will provide the resources to meet the study, instructional, informational, and normal research needs of its users, and that requests for materials from another library will be limited to unusual items <u>which the library does not own</u> and cannot readily obtain at moderate cost.... If an individual needs to use a large number of items located in another library, he or she should make arrangements to use them at that library.... The borrowing library is bound by any limitations on use imposed by the lending library.... Materials requested must be described completely and accurately following accepted bibliographic practice. Items requested should be verified and sources of verification given.... If this provision is disregarded and the bibliographic data appears to be incorrect, the request may be returned unfilled without special effort to identify the reference."

The Emerson College Library will request ILLs for faculty, staff, and graduate students, and for advanced undergraduates after consultation with library staff. We will request materials if they are related to reference, research, classwork, publication, etc., and if they fall within copyright guidelines (below).

We will locate through standard union lists local holders of materials and refer students to them. If a Fenway Consortium (FLC) library or the Boston Public Library holds an item, the student must visit the library in person. We will provide maps and direction to these libraries.

Copyright limitation: In each calendar year, we can request no more than 5 copies of articles from the most recent 5 years of any journal. This may be 5 copies of one article or 5 separate articles. If your request is number 6 during the year, we cannot send it, no matter what. There is no comparable limit for articles more than 5 years old, and there are no restrictions on articles from back issues of journals that we subscribe to.

We will place your request as quickly as possible, but please note that there are sometimes problems with computer down time and with slow mail delivery. ILLs will normally take at least 2 weeks, and may well take longer. Please allow enough time and plan ahead.

We do not charge other libraries for ILLs we loan to them, and to this date, we have not charged our faculty and students when the lending library has charged us a fee. We attempt to do our borrowing from other New England libraries who have signed a reciprocal agreement not to charge each other, and from the nationwide network of OCLC libraries who are willing to lend their holdings.

If you need an Interlibrary Loan, please contact the ILL Librarian or a Reference Librarian at 578-8675. We will be glad to discuss your ILL needs with you.

How to use

Interlibrary loan (ILL) is the borrowing and lending of materials between librari
over the world. When you need something that is not available in the Oberlin Cc
Libraries, you may fill out an Interlibrary Loan form at the Reference Desk to reques
the material be borrowed from another library.

WHO MAY USE INTERLIBRARY LOAN?

Oberlin College students, faculty, staff, faculty and staff spouses and people who li
work in Oberlin are eligible to use the ILL service, provided they first become regis
borrowers.

HOW LONG DOES ILL TAKE?

Usually you should allow two to three weeks for obtaining material you request. W
frequently get material more quickly, but you should not depend on having it so
than this. We submit most of our requests through an online computer system
allows us to send messages automatically to other institutions, but each item reque
still has to be sent through the mail. *Telefacsimile transmission (FAX) is reserved for ur
requests only.*

USING BORROWED MATERIALS

When the book or photocopy you have requested arrives, you will be notified by r
You may then pick up the item at the Circulation Desk in the Main Library. The len
library sets the loan period for books and also decides under what conditions they
be used. This may mean that you will be allowed to read the book in the Main Lib
only, especially if it is old or fragile.

HOW MUCH DOES ILL COST?

There is a 50¢ fee for each interlibrary loan request, whether it is for a loan or photoc
This must be paid at the time the request is made. Patrons who are not affiliated v
Oberlin College are charged an additional 15¢ per page for photocopies when the co
are picked up. FAX requests are $2. *Interlibrary Loan charges are non-refundable.* Pat
are advised to carefully verify that Oberlin does not own an item before submitti
request.

HOW TO MAKE AN ILL REQUEST

ILL request forms are available at the Reference Desk. Green forms are for photocop
yellow for loans. *Please fill out the form as carefully and completely as possible.* Complete
accurate information is necessary to fill your request. *The form must be submitted
member of the reference staff during posted reference desk hours.*

Latest Date I Can Use This:
Indicate the last date you can possibly use the item. Although requests are processed as quickly as possible, sometimes locating a copy can take several weeks, and there is no point in our continuing to try if you can no longer use it.

Source of Reference:
We need to know where you found your information about the book or article (bibliography, footnote, index). This ensures that the item exists and provides, if needed, a source for us to check your citation. Please provide as much information as possible.

Verification:
We ask you to help us verify the item by locating it in a standard bibliographical source, such as *Books in Print* for books, or *Ulrich's International Periodicals Directory* for periodicals. Please write the ISBN or LC card number, or the ISSN number for your item in the appropriate place on the request form. The Reference Librarian will assist you.

I certify...
To comply with the copyright law, we need your signature verifying that you intend to use the material for purposes of private study only.

SPECIAL MATERIALS

Periodicals:
Although it is usually easy for us to obtain photocopies of specific articles, most libraries will not lend entire issues or volumes of periodicals. We will try to request them, but cannot guarantee success.

Masters Theses:
List your reference as completely as possible on the request form, giving a source of reference if possible. Libraries that do not lend Masters theses will send us an estimate of the cost of purchasing microfilm and/or a photocopy. If you decide you want to pay the amount, the copy of the thesis would then be yours to keep.

PhD Dissertations:
You may ask at the Reference Desk to find out if a given university will lend its PhD dissertations, but many are available only by purchase from University Microfilms in Ann Arbor, Michigan. You should check *Comprehensive Dissertation Index* and *Dissertation Abstracts International* in the Reference Area for verification of your citation and the order number if you wish to purchase the dissertation. Ask at the Reference Desk for assistance.

WHAT ELSE SHOULD I KNOW ABOUT ILL?

We will make every attempt to secure a copy of the requested item. Sometimes it is difficult to borrow certain categories of material, such as reference books, textbooks, very new books, or very old or fragile materials. We may also be unable to locate the item. If we must make repeated requests through the mail, or if we cannot obtain the material you requested, we will notify you.

It is very important that we promptly return books borrowed through ILL. If you do not return a book on time, you will be charged a $5.00 overdue fee. If you do not return the book after subsequent warnings, you will be billed for the cost of the book's replacement and possibly other fees levied by the lending library.

ILL service slows down during the holiday season (usually December 12 – January 1) because most libraries don't wish to risk losing forms or items in the holiday mail. We do, however, continue to verify and find locations for material.

MWR, KL 7/91 rev.

Trinity College Library
Hartford, Connecticut

INTERLIBRARY LOAN AND PHOTOCOPY REQUEST POLICY

Trinity College Library
September, 1988

Interlibrary loan is a service offered by the Trinity College Library to aid faculty and students engaged in serious research. It is organized to complement the resources of the Trinity Library, not to supply the major part of materials needed for extended research.

Policies are based on the National Interlibrary Loan Code of the American Library Association and on the regulations of the individual lending libraries.

The time involved in processing interlibrary loan requests depends upon the nature of the material requested. Esoteric materials may take longer to identify and locate at another library, often taking up to four weeks, or even more, if they have to be pursued at several institutions. More common titles may be obtained within a shorter period of time. Most items will arrive within two weeks of their request.

We try to accomodate all research needs, but during especially busy periods, we reserve the right to limit the number of requests which may be submitted at any one time to four per person. The reason for this limitation is to allow access to as many people as possible to a heavily used service.

THE FOLLOWING MATERIALS ARE NOT GENERALLY AVAILABLE FO INTERLIBRARY LOAN:

1. Copies of titles that Trinity owns
2. Periodicals (Photocopies of specific articles may be requested. See section on photocopy requests.)
3. Reference books
4. Rare and other non-circulating books
5. Manuscripts
6. Pamphlets
7. Dissertations which are available through University Microfilms
8. Films, slides, phonograph records, and photographs
9. Material requiring expensive and difficult packing
10. Books to be put on reserve

PROCEDURE FOR REQUESTING A BOOK ON INTERLIBRARY LOAN

1. Check the CTW on-line computer catalog and the card catalog under author and title to be sure that the item is not available in the Trinity Library. If the item is in the CTW catalog but is not owned by Trinity, secure and fill out a request form at the Circulation desk.

2. For books not owned by Trinity, Wesleyan, or Connecticut College, fill out an interlibrary loan request form available at the Reference desk, supplying the author, title, publisher, place of publication, date, and any additional information which would be helpful in identifying the work. Please indicate where you found reference to the book, i.e., bibliography, footnote, etc. The more information you supply, the faster your request can be processed. Before sending requests to other libraries, we are required to verify your citation in standard bibliographic sources, and if your citation is incomplete, the processing of your request will be delayed.

3. You will be notified by campus mail when the requested material has arrived. It will be held for you at the Reference desk and can be retrieved any time that a professional librarian is on duty.

4. Interlibrary loan books from institutions other than Wesleyan or Connecticut College should be returned to the Reference desk, NOT the Circulation desk, on or before the due date. The due date is established by the lending library. Renewals may be granted in some cases if requested several days before the due date.

5. The fine for overdue interlibrary loan books is $.30 per day for the first thirty days and $1.00 per day thereafter up to a maximum fine of $50.00 per book. This fine schedule is necessary in order for us to maintain our borrowing privileges with other libraries. Our standing with the lending library is seriously jeopardized by our failure to return interlibrary loan material promptly.

Trinity College Library
Hartford, Connecticut

PROCEDURE FOR REQUESTING A PHOTOCOPIED ARTICLE THROUGH
INTERLIBRARY LOAN

1. Check the serials list to make sure the journal issue in
    which the article appears is not available here.

2. In consultation with a reference librarian, fill out a
    photocopy request form, available at the Reference desk,
    supplying periodical title, volume, and date, as well as
    author, title, and pages of the article.   Please indicate
    where you found reference to the article, i.e.,
    bibliography, index, abstract, footnote, etc.   The more
    information you supply, the faster your request can be
    processed. Before sending requests to other libraries , we
    are required to verify your citation in standard
    bibliographic sources, and if your citation is incomplete,
    the processing of your request will be delayed.

3. Be sure to indicate the maximum amount you are willing to
    spend for the photocopy. Your request form will be
    returned to you if you do not supply this information,
    thereby delaying the processing of your request.

4. The charge for photocopies varies according to the fee
    schedules of the supplying libraries. The charge for most
    of the copies that we receive from regional libraries is
    $1.00 minimum plus $.10 per page after the first ten pages.
    However, most other libraries have higher fees (a $5.00
    minimum plus a $.25 per page charge is not uncommon, and
    medical libraries charge $7.00), so you should be aware of
    the fact that some photocopies will cost more than the
    usual minimum of $1.00.

5. You will be notified by campus mail when the requested
    material has arrived. It will be held for you at the
    Reference desk and can be 'retrieved any time that a
    professional librarian is on duty.

INTERLIBRARY LOAN

MADDUX LIBRARY -- TRINITY UNIVERSITY
San Antonio, Texas

WHAT IS INTERLIBRARY LOAN?
Interlibrary Loan is a service which obtains study and research materials not available in the Maddux Library. Books are borrowed from other libraries, and photocopies of non-circulating materials can also be acquired. The conditions of this service are set by local agreements, the regulations of the individual lending libraries, and the National Interlibrary Loan Code.

WHO MAY USE INTERLIBRARY LOAN?
Current Trinity University students, faculty and staff are eligible.

HOW DO I USE INTERLIBRARY LOAN?
Simply fill out an Interlibrary Loan Request Form (available at both the Reference and Circulation Desks) as completely as possible, and turn it in at the Reference Desk during its service hours, or at the Circulation Desk at other times. When you want a periodical article, fill out a Periodical Interlibrary Loan Request (gray card). When you want a book, dissertation, report or government document, complete a Book Interlibrary Loan Request (brown card).

A postcard will be sent to notify you that the material has arrived and is available for you to pick up at the Circulation Desk.

HOW LONG DOES IT TAKE TO GET A BOOK OR PHOTOCOPY VIA INTERLIBRARY LOAN?
The time taken for requested materials to arrive depends upon several factors, including how close the supplying library is to Trinity, whether or not the item is immediately available at that library, and transit time. You should generally allow one to four weeks for receipt. IT IS IMPORTANT TO PLAN AHEAD WHEN REQUESTING MATERIALS ON INTERLIBRARY LOAN.

IS THERE A CHARGE FOR INTERLIBRARY LOAN?
There is usually no charge to students for materials received through ILL. Faculty and staff are charged only when a supplier charges the library and the cost is greater than $8.00. Rush delivery, when requested by the recipient, will be charged in full.

HOW LONG MAY I KEEP BOOKS?
The loan period is determined by the lending library and is usually two to three weeks. A renewal should be requested only when absolutely necessary and may be denied by the lending library. A renewal request must be made in advance of due date.

HOW DO I RETURN BORROWED MATERIALS?
All materials borrowed through interlibrary loan should be returned to the Maddux Library Circulation Desk. Please leave the yellow book sleeve attached. Late return of materials jeopardizes the ability of our library to borrow from other libraries in the future.

Revised September 1991

HOW TO EXPEDITE YOUR INTERLIBRARY LOAN REQUEST

The Maddux Library's Interlibrary Loan unit strives to process your requests as quickly as possible. However, during peak periods, more requests may be received than can normally be initiated within the same day. You can help us shorten the time required to process and fill your requests by following the guidelines listed below.
  During these busy periods, we will work first on those requests which follow these guidelines.
If you have questions about these points, please ask any member of the Reference staff.

FILLING OUT YOUR REQUEST CARD

1. Carefully check the Library's online catalog, TROILUS, to see if we own the item.
  (If our copy is missing or checked out, note that on the card.)

2. Print legibly.

3. Fill out the card as completely as possible.

4. Avoid all abbreviations.

5. Don't request an item when you are unsure of its correct citation. Ask the reference staff to help you.

6. Keep track of what you have requested and what dates you asked for them.

LOCATING LIBRARIES WHICH MAY OWN THE DESIRED ITEMS

For periodicals, check the *CORAL Union List of Periodicals* (at the Reference Desk) for local library holdings. If you locate the desired item, put the library name on the back side of the ILL card under "CORAL". For books published before 1987, check the *CORAL Union List of Monographs*.

For books or periodicals, check the OCLC terminal in Reference. OCLC is a computer database of over 20 million items. Instructions are located near the terminal; Reference staff can also help. If you find your item, note the OCLC number of the item on the back side of the ILL card.

Especially for older books, check the *National Union Catalog* (*NUC*) following the Z call numbers in the Reference collection. Note the *NUC* year, volume no., and page on your ILL card.

CHECKING ON THE STATUS OF A PREVIOUSLY REQUESTED ITEM

Ask first at the Circulation Desk; received items are held for you there. You will be sent a notification card for each item when it has been received in the library.

Wait at least 7 days after your request to ask the ILL staff, since status checks take time away from our efforts to acquire materials rapidly.

WHAT IS INTERLIBRARY LOAN ?

Books and periodicals not owned by Schaffer Library are
borrowed from other local, regional, national and
international libraries for use by Union's students,
faculty, staff and alumni.

Membership in the Captial District Library Council
(CDLC) enables us to borrow materials from more than
40 local libraries.

Through participation in a regional interlibrary loan
network ,NYSILL, we can borrow needed materials from
the major research libraries of New York State.

We routinely search the Online Computer Library Center
Database (OCLC) to locate and borrow materials owned
by other US, Canadian and European libraries.

WHAT MAY WE BORROW FOR YOU?

While we will try to borrow almost any item that is
requested, frequently we have problems borrowing:

    books still "in print" priced at $15 or less.
    books published with the last two years
    rare or fragile books
    multivolume sets
    reference books
    video cassettes
    theses/dissertations
    bound or single issue periodicals
    unpublished papers and reports
    compact discs
    computer software

ILL SCHAFFER LIBRARY UNION COLLEGE SCHENECTADY NY 12308
518-370-6282 or (FAX) 518-370-6619 (VAXMAIL) CAHILLM OR GLOVERC

Schaffer Library
Union College
Schenectady, New York

WHAT ARE COPYRIGHT RESTRICTIONS?

U.S. Copyright guidelines restrict the photocopying of copyrighted materials. There is an annual limit on the number of current periodical articles we can borrow from each journal title. Requests received after the limit is reached will be returned with instructions to consult the journal at a neighboring library. If the journal is not available locally, we will try to buy the article from a commercial document supplier.

BEFORE YOU MAKE A REQUEST

Check our library catalogs for book and periodical holdings. Check both the online and card catalogs.

Books that are not on the shelf may have been checked out. Periodicals may be in a shelving area. Check with the Circulation staff before requesting these items through ILL.

Have complete and accurate information about the book or article you need to borrow. Pagination for articles and publication dates for books are usually necessary. Keep a record of the source of your information.

MAKING A REQUEST

Forms for requesting books and periodicals are available at the Reference Desk. Use the 3x5 cards for book requests and the 5x8 for periodicals, newspapers, or other serial requests. Please print or write legibly and fill in all the blanks. **Provide the complete source of reference for any periodical requests.** Leave completed request forms in the bin at Reference.

HOW LONG WILL IT TAKE ?

We can often borrow books and periodical articles from local libraries within five business days. Items coming from out of state or those more difficult to verify or locate will take longer.

WHEN WILL THE BOOK BE DUE?

Each lending library sets its own due dates. This will
mean that even if you pick up several books on the
same day each one may have a different due date. A
card noting the borrowers name, date book was
received in the library and date the book is due will be
placed in the book.

Renewals are also controlled by the lending library.
Request a renewal at least five days before the due
date. Please do not request renewals by phone, come to
the ILL office or contact us via VAXMAIL or FAX.

Overdue fines are charged for all late books. We have a
liberal four days "grace" period after which time the
fine charged is $.25 per day.for each overdue book.

HOW WILL I BE NOTIFIED?

Notices will be sent to your campus mail address. If you have a VAX
Mail account, notification can be sent to your VAX mail address. Please note
your VAX address on the request card.

Please feel free to check at anytime about the status of your
requests. The Interlibrary Loan office is open from 8:30 AM to 4:30 PM
Monday through Friday. We are located in the office at the end of the
Bibliography Reference Room. If you wish to reach us by phone please call
the number listed below. You may also send messages through VAX Mail to
Mary Cahill, address is CAHILLM or Christine Glover, address is GLOVERC.

Books and periodical articles borrowed for you will be held at the
Reference Desk. Please arrange to pick them up promptly. Please return
books borrowed through ILL to the Reference Desk or Interlibrary Loan
Office. Reproductions of periodical articles are yours to keep.

GOOD NEWS!

Schaffer Library
Union College
Schenectady, New York

IS THERE A CHARGE?

Generally, there is no charge to our patrons for materials borrowed through ILL. The library, however, is often charged by providing libraries for postage, mailing, photoduplication charges, and loan fees,etc.. At this time these fees are subsidized by various library funds

To help us keep costs down please try to : pick up items promptly, avoid reordering books -- use them well the first time, make a record of what you have requested so that you don't order duplicates; and,if your topic changes or you have no more need for the items you requested, please let us know!

ELECTRONIC TRANSMISSION OF ILL REQUESTS

Soon we will be accepting requests for Interlibrary Loan via VAX MAIL -- watch for details!

SAMPLE FORMS FOR ILL REQUESTS

INTERLIBRARY LOAN REQUEST - PERIODICAL/JOURNAL
(Always check serial catalogue before submitting request)

Periodical Title _Life Magazine_

Volume _5_ No _Title 1982_ Pages _43-45_

Author _Press, Arthur_ Title of Article _Good life at 50._

Verification (in what source did you find this article cited?)
Index _Readers Guide_ Year,Vol&Page _1982 V.42 p 617_
Accession No _____ Other _____

Your Name _Noone, Jim_ Box/Office No _6623_
Address _VAX_ Phone No _377-7671_

Notice:Warning Concerning Copyright Restriction:The copyright law of the US(Title 17,US Code) governs the making of photocopies or other reproduction of copyrighted material.Under certain conditions specified in law,libraries and archives are authorized to furnish photocopy or other reproduction. One of these specified conditions is that the photocopy or reproduction is not to be used for any purpose other than private study, scholarship or research. If a user makes a request for, or later uses, a photocopy or reproduction for purposes in excess of "fair use," that user may be liable for copyright infringement. This institution reserves the right to refuse to accept a copying order if, in its judgement, fulfillment of the order would involve violation of copyright law. (OCLC #)

INTERLIBRARY LOAN REQUEST - BOOK
Author _Zegbedlor, Harriet_
(Last Name First!)
Title _Death on the Tennis Court_

Publisher _Harper_ Date Published _19_
Your name _Public, J._ Phone _66_
Box # OR Dept. & Bldg. _A134_
Can't use after _2/17/90_ UNION CO
(Office use) OCLC #:

Guide to Resources

UWS Interlibrary Loan Policy

1. Interlibrary Loan services are available through the Jim Dan Hill Library for faculty, staff, and students of UW-Superior. Other patrons should contact their local public library for Interlibrary Loan services. Questions regarding UWS Interlibrary Loan policies or procedures should be directed to the Interlibrary Loan department at 394-8130.

2. Interlibrary Loan materials can be requested by filling out a UWS Interlibrary Loan card as completely and legibly as possible. Periodical titles, names, article titles, and publishing information should not be abbreviated. Interlibrary Loan cards should be turned in to the Jim Dan Hill Public Services Desk for processing.

3. The length of time needed to obtain an Interlibrary Loan can vary depending on the request, but patrons should allow a minimum of ten days for the completion of a request. (See flow chart on back) Some requests, particularly for books, can take considerably longer to obtain.

4. An attempt will be made to notify the requester when Interlibrary Loan materials arrive, but it is ultimately the responsibility of the patron to follow up on the request. If the request has not arrived in a reasonable amount of time, an Interlibrary Loan staff member should be consulted to determine the status of the request.

5. Photocopies of periodical article requests usually become the property of the requester. Due dates for books or non-print materials borrowed from another library must be honored as part of the Interlibrary Loan resource-sharing agreement. **No renewal is possible for borrowed materials.**

6. Most libraries will not loan audio-visual materials. Patrons should consult an Interlibrary Loan staff member when attempting to order audio-visual materials.

7. Materials published within the past 12 months may not be available through Interlibrary Loan.

8. The requester is responsible for any replacement charges assessed by the lending library for Interlibrary Loan materials that are damaged or overdue.

Hill Library
University of Wisconsin-Superior
Superior, Wisconsin

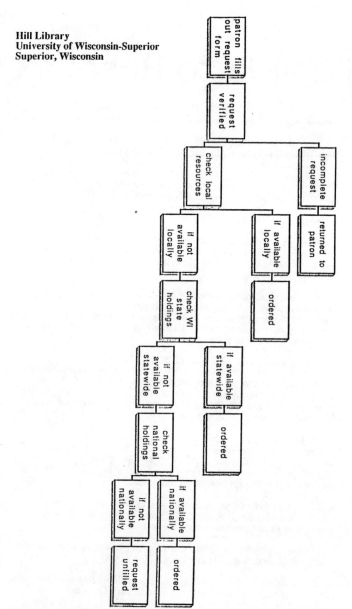

SPECIAL POLICIES

FACULTY INTERLIBRARY LOAN POLICY
Roux Library - Florida Southern College

BORROWING POLICY

Research materials not available in Roux Library may be obtained through Interlibrary Loan. Roux Library actively participates as a borrower and lender in the Tampa Bay Library Consortium (TBLC) and Florida Library Information Network (FLIN) programs. Both programs encourage free sharing of library resources used for research, and every attempt is made to secure loans from member libraries.

Although libraries will not loan periodicals, photocopies of articles may be obtained. The library pays Interlibrary Loan photocopy charges up to $5.00 per request, for faculty members and students.

BORROWING PROCEDURE

Requests for loans may be placed at the Circulation Desk. A separate request form must be submitted for each item, and complete citations and source of the reference should be provided. Please read and sign the notice concerning copyright compliance for each request.

Interlibrary loans are usually received within two weeks from the date of request. Books available from TBLC or FLIN libraries often arrive more quickly.

A notice is placed in the faculty member's mailbox when a book has been received, and the book may be picked up at the Circulation Desk. Photocopies of journal articles are placed directly in the mailbox.

LENGTH OF LOAN

The length of loan is established by the lending library, and books must be returned promptly. Failure to do so will jeopardize the Library's borrowing privileges with other institutions. The due date will be prominently displayed on all items which must be returned. Renewal requests should be made four days prior to the due date at the Circulation Desk.

QUESTIONS?

Please do not hesitate to contact the library regarding local availability of library materials, and for more details about Interlibrary Loan services. Our phone number is 680-4164.

University of South Carolina-Spartanburg Library
Spartanburg, South Carolina

USCS
INTERLIBRARY LOAN
DISSERTATION REQUEST POLICY

Dissertations may be available from the University at which the dissertation was completed. The lending policy of these libraries varies considerably. Some lend willingly at no cost, some lend for a fee (usually about $10.00) and others will not lend under any circumstances.

When requesting a dissertation you may specify that you wish to borrow only if free or, by signing the ILL form, you may agree to a charge up to $10.00 (not $8.00 as for ordinary ILL requests). You will be charged only if the lending library charges USCS.

If the dissertation in which you are interested is not available for borrowing through ILL, then you may be able to purchase it from UMI. You may telephone UMI (University Microfilms International) to determine availability. (1-800-521-0600). They will need the author's name, title, degree date and university. The cost is approximately $25.00 for microfilm and $35.00 for a paper copy plus shipping and handling. UMI will require payment in advance.

Estep Library
Southwest Baptist University
Bolivar, Missouri

Adopted August 1990
Revised February 1992
Review Annually

Policy on

Provision of Periodical Articles

Due to the increasing cost of periodical subscriptions, the Southwest Baptist University Library canceled subscriptions to some of the most costly, less used journals. Rising costs also prohibit adding many subscriptions. In order to provide periodical articles from journals to which the library does not subscribe, the following policy will be in effect:

1. Any student needing an article from a journal to which the library does not subscribe may request a free copy of the article. This request must be accompanied by the signature of the faculty member of the class for which the article is needed, and the signature of a librarian to insure that the student has examined and made use of relevant materials already owned by the library (see attached form). Beginning August 1992, the student will pay only the $.10 per page photocopy cost while the library will pay all other costs associated with acquiring the article.

2. Seven to ten days are required for receipt of the article by mail. If the student wishes to receive the article in less time by the use of telefacsimile transmission, the student must pay the fax charges involved (see attached form).

In order to provide this service and remain within copyright guidelines, the library will utilize an acceptable clearinghouse service which pays royalty fees, when more than five articles have been requested from a journal within the year (August-July). Regular interlibrary loan channels will be utilized until the five articles from a given journal title have been obtained as allowed by copyright guidelines.

The cost of obtaining these articles will be paid out of library funds in lieu of subscribing to expensive journals for which there is limited demand. If at any time the cost of providing articles equals or exceeds the cost of the subscription, the library will consider entering a subscription to the periodical.

articles.pol

CENTRAL COLLEGE LRC INTERLIBRARY LOAN FAX POLICY

The LRC belongs to national, regional and local consortia which attempt to provide low-cost, equitable interlibrary loan service to member libraries. Libraries use well-established methods of submitting requests for information via telecommunications or mails and sending materials via ground or air transportation. FAX as a means of borrowing and lending is a newer method and has not been fully standardized. The cost and unreliability of telefacsimile transmission are factors to be considered in making requests. Nonetheless, the LRC will attempt to respond to patrons and libraries desiring that photocopies of materials be FAXed. The LRC expects that requests for materials to be FAXed are by their very nature made for items that are so important and urgently needed that they should receive special attention; and further that the normal 2 to 3 week delivery time is unacceptable.

Service to Central College LRC Patrons

Normally the LRC receives photocopies via US mails. However, when librarians determine that students, faculty or staff involved in research have legitimate time constraints, librarians will request that photocopies be FAXed to the College. Patrons should realize that attention to Central's requests are dependent on the lending library's ability and willingness to give "rush" service to our requests. Therefore, materials may not be received sooner than 3 to 5 days even though FAX is requested.

Patrons will not be charged for FAX service.

Service to Other Libraries

The following guidelines will be used by the LRC in providing FAX service to other libraries:

1. The LRC accepts FAXed ILL requests for materials. Borrowing libraries should make every effort to use standardized formats such as ALA forms or OCLC information when requesting materials.

2. The LRC will notify the library by FAX if a request cannot be filled.

3. The LRC will mail or FAX photocopies to borrowing libraries according to the borrowing library's request.

4. Under normal circumstances, the LRC will FAX photocopies within 48 hours, excluding weekends and holidays.

5. Maximum number of pages for one article that the LRC will FAX is 15.

6. The LRC does not charge borrowing libraries for FAX service.

7. The LRC is a partner in the State of Iowa Net Lender Reimbursement Program.

11-28-90
rem

EXCERPTS FROM LIBRARY
HANDBOOKS

Fishburn Library Handbook

INTERLIBRARY LOAN

In doing your research, you may find citations for books or journal articles which are not available at Fishburn Library. Interlibrary loan (ILL, for short) gives you access to the collections at hundreds of academic (and public) libraries in the U.S.

Book loans

You may borrow books, bound periodicals, and music scores through ILL. (Reference books, recordings, and old or rare books generally are not circulated on ILL.)

PLAN AHEAD!! The items you request will be _mailed_ to us from the lending institution. Thus you should allow one to two weeks for a book to arrive at Fishburn. Since items ordered at the same time will probably arrive at the same time, and be due at the same time, it is often a good idea to stagger your requests if your list is a long one.

Loan periods for ILL items vary from two to four weeks. There is a $10 fine for overdue items. Books are also subject to recall by the lending library. If you receive a recall notice, return the book immediately; we will try to get another copy from a different library.

Articles

You may request photocopies of periodical articles through ILL. Since the photocopies will be yours to keep, there is no need to stagger requests if you have a long list. There is a fee for photocopying -- usually 10 cents per page. Some institutions now charge a $2 to $5 minimum. If you wish to restrict costs, please note your limit on the request form.

PLAN AHEAD! It takes one to two weeks for orders to arrive.

How to make ILL requests

The procedure for making ILL requests is straightforward:

1) Double check: Are you sure we don't have the item(s)? Ask for help if you're uncertain where something may be located.

2) Fill out the _appropriate_ form. These forms are available in the Reference Office (or make copies from the samples on the next page). In filling out the form, be as specific as possible, and include all of the required information. For photocopy requests, be sure to write out the entire title of the periodical -- don't use the short form given in the index citation. Also, give the title and year of the index you used and the number of the page on which the citation is listed.

3) Leave the completed form in the wire basket on the shelf in the Reference Office. You will be notified when your item arrives.

H. Raymond Danforth Library
New England College
Henniker, New Hampshire

WHAT WE DON'T HAVE AND WHERE TO FIND IT

It is naturally impossible to have everything you might need or want to use in one library. Therefore, we have "connections". New England College is a member institution of the New Hampshire College and University Council (NHCUC). One of the advantages of this membership is the access we have to the libraries of all other members. You, as an NEC student, have two options for using this system.

Direct borrowing: By going to any member library and showing your college ID card, you may check out materials directly from that library. We provide a service through NEC's Danforth Library for returning these books. NHCUC members are:

> Colby-Sawyer College, New London
> Daniel Webster College, Nashua
> *Dartmouth College, Hanover
> Franklin Pierce College, Rindge
> Keene State College, Keene
> New Hampshire College, Manchester
> Plymouth State College, Plymouth
> Rivier College, Nashua
> St. Anselm College, Manchester
> University of New Hampshire, Durham
> University of New Hampshire at Manchester

*Dartmouth College restricts use of its libraries; ask the reference librarian for details.

Interlibrary Loan (I.L.L.): You may request materials at the NEC library that we do not own. We then process this request so that not only NHCUC libraries are tapped, but also all major libraries in the state. (In this way you have access to more than 4 million books and a vast number of periodicals).

H. Raymond Danforth Library
New England College
Henniker, New Hampshire

Although current guidelines for implementing the new copyright law may affect your request, usually, if the item you want is available, you will be lent the book or given a photocopy of the article. If you don't know specific items to request, check with a reference librarian. He or she can usually show you how to find what you need.

Things to remember:

1. The I.L.L. process takes time. Many factors affect how long it takes to fill your request, but try to allow **at least two weeks** between when you ask for something and when you plan to use it.

2. Generally speaking, materials are available only if owned by a library in the state of New Hampshire.

3. We can request something on I.L.L. **only** if the NEC library does **not** own it.

4. Try to give as much information as possible for each request. We are not being picky. It truly helps us to help you if we know authors' (full) names, titles, publication dates, pages, and the sources of your reference. These questions appear on the forms we ask you to fill out for I.L.L. service.

5. Please be prompt in picking up and returning I.L.L. books. You will be notified when materials are here and when they are due. Note that you are responsible for overdue fines and other charges from the lending library, if applicable.

6. Please see a reference librarian for any questions you have. We are here to help you!

Oesterle Library
North Central College
Naperville, Illinois

OBTAINING MATERIALS FROM OTHER LIBRARIES

Patron Category	Interlibrary Loan?	Borrow in person from ILCSO libraries?	Borrow in person from LIBRAS libraries?
Students	yes	yes	yes
Faculty, emeritus faculty & exempt staff	yes	yes	yes
Nonexempt staff	yes	yes	yes
Trustees, Donor's Club members & faculty spouses	yes	yes	no
Nichols/public library patrons, alumni & former students	no	no	no

Interlibrary Loan:

Interlibrary loan requests for materials are made by filling out the appropriate request form and returning it to the Circulation Desk. Incomplete, illegible or inaccurate information on interlibrary loan forms delays the processing of requests; please ask a library staff member if you need assistance in filling out forms.

Books: Books may be borrowed from the 40 ILCSO libraries which are members of Illinet Online by filling out a blue "Interlibrary Loan Request for an LCS Book." If the original lending library cannot supply the material, the interlibrary loan staff will reorder the book from another library. Books can also be borrowed from non-ILCSO libraries; for more information, contact a library staff member.

Photocopies: Photocopies of journal articles not in Oesterle Library's periodicals collection may be requested by filling out a yellow "Interlibrary Loan Request for Photocopy."

There is a charge of $ .10 per page for photocopies. In some instances a supplier will charge more than this amount. If you agree on the request form to pay more than $.10 per page for photocopies, you will be required to pay this higher price if the supplier charge a higher per-page rate. You are responsible for paying for all photocopies received.

Title 17, United States Code stipulates that institutions may not borrow more than five articles from recent issues (five years old or newer) of a single periodical title which the borrowing library does not own. If a request puts the library over its legal limit for the title requested, the interlibrary loan staff will furnish you with a list of libraries holding the material.

rev. 9/91

HOW DOES INTERLIBRARY LOAN WORK?

We are part of the River Bend Library System, which runs a daily pick-up-delivery service, Mondays through Friday. Our most immediate resources are the local college, public and special libraries. Thus, if you need a periodical article, and our Quad Cities Union List of Serials (on reserve at the desk by the front door) tells us that Augustana has it, you can fill out a photocopy request form and the librarian will call over to Augie and ask the librarians there to copy it. It will be delivered, free of charge, on the next delivery day. The same time frame applies if books you want are available locally. If they are not available locally, the library system will forward the request to various libraries owning those items. Delivery in that case could reasonably be expected to take two weeks or more; thus the system will be of most use to those who begin research on their papers early.

The service is generally free, but when charges are made by the lending library, we pass them on to the borrower. If you do not want to pay photocopy charges, state that on the photocopy request form you fill out. While most material we borrow is delivered at no cost, if you wish to guarantee getting the material you should indicate a willingness to pay up to $7.50.

CONSORTIA POLICIES

CENTRAL NEW YORK LIBRARY RESOURCES COUNCIL
REGIONAL INTERLIBRARY LOAN CODE

ADOPTED BY THE BOARD OF TRUSTEES - JULY 28, 1987

The function of the Central New York Library Resources Council's Regional Interlibrary Loan Code is to establish policy for and to facilitate interlibrary loan among CENTRO's member institutions. CENTRO's ILL policy is based upon the ALA National Interlibrary Loan Code, (New York, 1980). A copy follows.

CENTRO's mission statement (revised 1/28/86) recognizes the need "to improve reference and research library services in the Central New York region." A major goal is "to insure that needed information resources are made available as required by researchers in the region," by encouraging the expansion of interlibrary loan traffic within the region, and utilizing to the fullest extent possible, other interlibrary loan networks. (Goal II, and Goal II, Objective C)

CENTRO's ILL history among its member institutions has been marked by an extremely liberal openness between suppliers and borrowers. Access to members' collections is a major condition when joining the Council. Access among CENTRO members is defined as the privilege of any member library or system to receive ILL materials from any other member on a mutually non-restrictive, non-fee basis. The Council's past practice and policy has been to facilitate interlibrary loan access by subsidizing the delivery program for members.

Many aspects of CENTRO's liberal ILL access history have been adhered to without much discussion or any firm written guidelines. In order to delineate CENTRO members' interlibrary loan responsibilities within the Council, the following points are agreed upon:

* All ILL requests are considered legitimate requests for information and are treated equally regardless of source of request.

* There are no unreasonable quantitative restrictions on the loan of items. However, the Council encourages members to distribute their ILL activity across the Council membership where possible and not to burden any single library.

* In keeping with the current NYSL photocopy policy, the first 33 pp. are provided free, regardless of storage medium (hard copy, microform, laser disc, etc.) Requests exceeding 33 pp. may be provided free-of-charge, dependent on the lender's policy.

* Fullest bibliographic verification should be provided.

* Full OCLC members input and maintain ILL policies in OCLC's Name-Address Directory. For non-full OCLC participants the Bib Center enters and maintains ILL policies in the NAD. It is the borrower's responsibility to check and adhere to the lender's policies as stated in the NAD.

* ILL statistics are submitted each month to the CENTRO office on provided forms.

* Members provide other such information as may be required by CENTRO in support of its ILL programs.

* SUNY Health Science Center Library as a Regional Medical Library (RML) is the only member which charges in the form of RML coupons for ILL requests. CENTRO disseminates RML coupons to members.

CENTRO's ILL program is coordinated by the Bibliographic Services Coordinator. The ILL/Delivery Committee serves as an advisory body reporting to the Executive Director.

Non-compliance with any or all of a member institution's interlibrary loan responsibilities is a serious matter. It could precipitate a review by the ILL/Delivery Committee and a recommendation to the Executive Director for consideration by the Board of Trustees resulting in possible loss of membership benefits.

SUNY/OCLC Network

Interlibrary Loan Agreement

This Code is a voluntary agreement to govern all interlibrary lending among libraries in the SUNY/OCLC Network. It is intended to promote a more liberal interlibrary loan policy among the libraries adopting it than that of the ALA National Interlibrary Loan Code. This code is based on the premise that lending among libraries for the use of an individual is in the public interest and should be encouraged.

I. Definition

Interlibrary loans are transactions in which library materials or copies of library materials are made available by one library to another upon request.

II. Scope

Under the terms of this agreement, any type of library material may be requested on loan or in photocopy from another library. The lending library retains the right of deciding in each case whether a particular item should or should not be provided, and whether the original or a copy should be sent.

III. Responsibility of Borrowing Libraries

A. It is recognized that interlibrary lending does not relieve any library of the responsibility of developing its own collection. Each library should provide the resources to meet the ordinary study, educational, instructional, informational and research needs of its users. No library should depend upon another to supply the recurring needs of its clients.

B. Participants in this agreement, where feasible and cost effective, should follow local, regional or state cooperative resource sharing agreements, taking care to avoid concentrating the burden of requests on a few libraries. Local resources should be exhausted before going to other members.

C.   The borrowing library is responsible for compliance with the copyright law (Title 17, U.S. Code) and its accompanying guidelines, and should inform its users of the applicability of the law. An indication of compliance must be provided with all copy requests.

D.   The safety of borrowed material is the responsibility of the borrowing library from the time the material leaves the lending library until it is returned to the lending library. The borrowing library is responsible for packaging the material so as to insure its return in good condition. If damage or loss occurs, the borrowing library must meet all costs of repair or replacement, in accordance with the preference of the lending library.

E.   The borrowing library and its users must comply with the conditions of loan established by the lending library. All material on loan is subject to immediate recall, and the borrowing library shall comply promptly.

F.   The borrowing library agreeing to abide by this code should place "@/S" in the cost area of the interlibrary loan form used.

IV.   Responsibility of Lending Libraries

A.   The decision to loan material is at the discretion of the lending library. SUNY/OCLC members are encouraged, however, to interpret as generously as possible their own lending policy with due consideration to the interest of their primary clientele.

B.   A statement of interlibrary loan policy and charges will be provided to other libraries either online or in writing upon request. This statement should be reviewed annually.

C. A lending library is responsible for informing any borrowing library of its apparent failure to follow the provision of this code.

D. A lending library will not require information about the status of the individual for whom material is being requested.

V. Expenses

A. SUNY/OCLC member libraries who sign this agreement will not charge each other for the following:

1. Fees for handling interlibrary loan requests

2. Postage or other transportation charges exclusive of telefacsimile costs

3. Photocopying (up to 33 pages per request)

4. Insurance

B. The borrowing library should be prepared to assume costs for lost and damaged materials and any other costs not excluded by this code.

VI. Violation of the Code

Each library is responsible for maintaining the provisions of this code in good faith.

VII. Withdrawal from the Code

If the participating library wishes to withdrawal from this agreement, a statement in writing to that effect should be submitted to the SUNY/OCLC Network 30 days prior to the anticipated date of withdrawal.

STATE REIMBURSEMENT AGREEMENT

LETTER OF AGREEMENT
Iowa Interlibrary Loan Program

To encourage and support multitype resource sharing through interlibrary loan, the State Library of Iowa is offering a net lender reimbursement program to Iowa libraries.

The _____ Wartburg College _____ Library agrees to participate in the Iowa Interlibrary Loan Program from October 1, 1989, through June 30, 1990, in accord with the guidelines listed below. The State Library of Iowa agrees to provide net lender compensation to the participating libraries in accord with the terms of the guidelines below.

Guidelines:

1. This program is based on reciprocity, the sharing of resources. Each participating library must be willing to lend materials to other Iowa libraries. To facilitate this, each library must contribute MARC records of its holdings to the state database, the Iowa Locator.

2. Reimbursement will be for the number of net lending transactions, that is, the total number of items loaned to other Iowa libraries during the period of this agreement less the total number of items received from other Iowa libraries.

3. The lending library will assess no interlibrary loan charge for either the borrowing library or the end user. Prohibited interlibrary loan charges (assessed by either the lending library or the borrowing library) would include service charges, use charges, telecommunications charges, postage, etc. However, charges for damaged or lost materials are not consider interlibrary loan charges.

4. The lending library will follow its own policy regarding the charge to the borrowing library for lost or damaged materials. The borrowing library, in accord with its own policy, will collect this amount from the responsible patron. The State Library will not provide reimbursement for materials lost or damaged through interlibrary loan.

5. Only items loaned to Iowa libraries are eligible for this reimbursement program. Eligible libraries are public libraries (including the State Library), college and university libraries, community college and area school libraries, elementary and secondary school media centers, and AEA media centers. Only items borrowed from Iowa libraries are counted in the calculation of the net lending total.

6. During this initial year, special libraries are not eligible to participate in this program. This means that items loaned to special libraries (business libraries, hospital libraries, law libraries, governmental agency libraries, etc.) cannot be included in the calculation of a net lending total.

7. Any type of library material can be included in the count of interlibrary loan transactions (books, periodicals, photocopies of library materials sent by mail, copies of library materials sent by telefax, audio tapes, video tapes, films, etc.). A copy of an article or a copy of a number of pages from one book would be counted as one interlibrary loan transaction. Each lending library will follow its own policies regarding the lending of nonprint materials and noncirculating materials.

8. Requests for interlibrary loans can be placed in any convenient manner acceptable to the lending library (ICAN, OCLC, other electronic mail programs, fax, telephone calls, mail, etc.). Lending libraries will count all lending transactions equally regardless of how they received the request. When sending requests, libraries will follow the appropriate, existing protocol for ICAN, OCLC, the Regional Libraries, or any other special agreement.

9. Requesting libraries may send interlibrary loan requests via fax but will request only materials from known locations (e.g., periodicals included in a union list of serials). If there are several known locations, the following protocol will be observed:
   a) Send request first to the known library location in same community.
   b) Send request to library of same type (e.g. public library to public library) considering:
      1) Geographic proximity (normally closest library first)
      2) Size of library (normally smallest library first in order to distribute the lending responsibility).
   c) Send request to other types of libraries, again considering geographic proximity and size of library.

10. The State Library's reimbursement of net lending must be used to supplement, not replace local funding support, or the library will not be eligible for net lending reimbursement. This applies to all types of libraries participating in the agreement.

11. The State Library's reimbursement of net lending will not replace state funds distributed through the Iowa Regional Library System. The public libraries that are regional resource centers (including the distributed resource center libraries in the Central Region) are not eligible for this program.

12. AEA Media Centers already are funded to provide service to schools. Thus, an AEA media center's total number of items loaned cannot include items sent to teachers or to school media centers. Items that an AEA media center sends to public libraries or academic libraries are eligible for net lender reimbursement.

Participating libraries will report monthly statistics and make claims for payment in accord with directions and deadlines established by the State Library. Lending libraries will send to the State Library verification of loans (e.g., copies of ALA request forms). The detailed statistics available through the ICAN and OCLC programs are sufficient verification for these transactions.

When the State Library receives the final statistics for the period of time covered by this agreement, the total funds available for this program will be divided by the total number of net lending transactions to determine the precise rate of reimbursement. Thus, please note that reimbursement will occur after July 1, 1990.

___Wartburg College___ **Library**	**State Library of Iowa**
_____**Federal ID**	
Employer Number	
[signature] **Signature**	_____
___Library Director___ **Title**	**Shirley George,**
10/19/89	**State Librarian of Iowa**

RECIPROCAL AGREEMENT
REQUEST FORMS

HIO · WESLEYAN ·

Ohio Wesleyan University
Delaware, Ohio 43015
Telephone 614-369-4431

AGREEMENT:

Ohio Wesleyan University Libraries (OWU) will provide free photocopies to your library with the understanding that you will extend the same considerations to us. It is understood that either library may terminate this agreement at any time by providing written notice. If these arrangements are acceptable to you, please complete the section below and return one copy to us.

ibrary name & mailing address:

_____   Beeghly Library (and branches)

_____   Ohio Wesleyan University

_____   Delaware, Ohio 43015

_____

CLC symbol: _____   OCLC symbol: __OWU__

uthorized by: Authorized by:

ame: _____   Name: _____

itle: _____   Title: _____

ate: _____   Date: _____

For those libraries that charge for book loans, would you also be interested in extending this agreement to include book loans?
                                        yes_____   no_____

Thanks for your time. Please return completed form to Beeghly Library (OWU).

Krannert Memorial Library
University of Indianapolis
Indianapolis, Indiana

University of Indianapolis

1400 East Hanna Avenue
Indianapolis, Indiana 46227-3697

Krannert Memorial Library

(317) 788-32

INTERLIBRARY LOAN RECIPROCAL AGREEMENT

The University of Indianapolis Krannert Memorial Library (III) will provide your library with free photocopies and free loans in exchange for the same privileges to our requests.

This agreement may be cancelled by either library at any time upon prior written notification.

If this arrangement is acceptable to you, please complete the section below and return it to the following address:

> Mrs. Christine Guyonneau
> University of Indianapolis
> Krannert Memorial Library
> Reference Department
> 1400 East Hanna Avenue
> Indianapolis, IN 46227

_____

_____Library agrees to provide free photocpies and free loans to the University of Indianapolis Krannert Memorial Library on a reciprocal basis.

Institution Name_____

OCLC Symbol_____   FAX Number_____ Tel. _____

Authorized Name and Signature_____

Title_____   Date_____

112 - Reciprocal Agreement Request Forms

INTERLIBRARY LOAN FORMS

IMPORTANT! SEE BACK OF FORM!

INTERLIBRARY LOAN REQUEST
Abilene Christian University

INCOMPLETE REQUESTS WILL NOT BE PROCESSED!

Name _____ Date _____

Address _____

Phone _____

Status _____ Department _____

Is this available in HSU, McM or APL libraries? _____

rce of reference [title (no acronyms), vol., year, page or abstract no.]: _____

ABBREVIATIONS

iodical title _____

cle title _____

ume _____ Number _____ Month _____ Year _____ Pages _____

k title _____

thor _____ Publisher _____ Year _____

nderstand there will be at least a $1 charge for this material.

Maximum amount
willing to

nature _____ ☐ Cash ☐ Dept. Acct. _____ pay $_____

IMPORTANT! SEE BACK OF FORM!

Brown Library
Abilene Christian University
Abilene, Texas

INTERLIBRARY LOAN (ILL)

I. Who may use the interlibrary loan service?
   A. Faculty/staff.
   B. Graduates.
   C. Undergraduates with their professor's co-signature on the ILL request card.

II. How long does it take?
   A. Average time: two weeks.
   B. Requests should be turned in on a properly filled out request card at least four weeks before date needed.
      REQUESTS WITHOUT ADEQUATE INFORMATION WILL NOT BE PROCESSED.
   C. "Difficult to research" items may take longer than two weeks delivery time.

III. What can be received through ILL?
   A. Books which must be returned on time and in good condition.
   B. Photocopies of articles which may be kept by patron.

IV. How much does it cost?
   A. ACU Library charges $1 for our services.
   B. The lending library may also charge for their services. These fees range from $1 to $15.
   C. Average cost to patron is $1. PAYABLE UPON RECEIPT OF MATERIAL.
   D. Patrons who do not pick up their ILL materials will still be charged for the service.

INTERLIBRARY LOAN REQUEST FORM

PLEASE FILL IN BOTH SIDES

FROM: Aurora University Library   TO:
        347 South Gladstone
        Aurora, IL 60506-4892
        Phone: 708-844-5437
        Fax #:   708-892-9286

BOOK   PERIODICAL

Title_____   Periodical Title_____

_____   _____

Author_____   Vol._____#____Date_____

Edition_____Year_____   Pages_____

Publisher_____ .   Author_____

                                           Title/Article_____

                                           _____

**Where did you find the above information?_____

/ /108(g)(2)Guidelines (CCG)   / /other provisions (CCL)

Charles B. Phillips Library
Aurora University
Aurora, Illinois

PLEASE FILL IN BOTH SIDES

Patron Name_____Date_____

Social Security #_____Phone_____

Not needed after_____

Remember it is your responsibility to ask the circulation desk
assistant if your items have arrived. You will be billed for
photocopies received but not picked up. There is a 10 cent per page
charge for photocopies and a limit of 5 requests per day.

Your Signature_____

****
Office use only

Date Requested_____

Date Received_____

Date Due_____

Date Returned_____

CIDENTAL COLLEGE
RARY
s Angeles, California

INTERLIBRARY LOAN
[REQUEST FORM]

PLEASE PRINT CLEARLY. • DO NOT USE ABBREVIATIONS. • ONLY 1 REQUEST PER FORM.
• FILL IN ONE SECTION COMPLETELY.

ase check OASys Catalog and with the Reference Librarian before submitting a request.

ne: _____ Date: _____

al Address/Box: _____ Phone: _____

☐ FACULTY   ☐ OXY STUDENT   ☐ ADMINISTRATOR/STAFF
EPT./COURSE: _____   CANCEL IF NOT RECEIVED BY: _____

SECTION I: ☐ BOOK   ☐ DISSERTATION   ☐ SCORE   ☐ RECORDING   OTHER _____

AUTHOR: _____

ITLE: _____

PUBLISHER: _____ YEAR _____

WHERE WAS THIS ITEM MENTIONED? _____

SECTION II: MAGAZINE/JOURNAL ARTICLE

AUTHOR: _____

ARTICLE TITLE: _____

JOURNAL TITLE: _____

VOL._____   ISSUE: _____   DATE: _____   PAGES: _____

WHERE WAS THIS ITEM MENTIONED? _____
Required by lending library for verification.

Warning Concerning Copyright Restrictions

- -

or library use only

		Request Mode
		Manual ☐ OCLC ☐

SBN/ISSN: _____   OCLC: _____

_____ ILL#: _____

enders: _____

Date Req'd: _____   Date Rec'd: _____   DEL. TIME: _____

Due Date: _____   Date Ret'd: _____

OCCIDENTAL COLLEGE
LIBRARY
Los Angeles, California

INTERLIBRARY LOAN
(NOTIFICATION FORM)

PHONE

Date:_____

Your Interlibrary Loan request ☐ has arrived and is being held for you at the Circulation D

☐ has not been located. Contact ILL for more information.

Name: _____ Date: _____

Local Address/Box: _____ Phone: _____

☐ FACULTY ☐ OXY STUDENT ☐ ADMINISTRATOR/STAFF
DEPT./COURSE: _____ CANCEL IF NOT RECEIVED BY: _____

SECTION I: ☐ BOOK ☐ DISSERTATION ☐ SCORE ☐ RECORDING OTHER _____

AUTHOR: _____

TITLE: _____

PUBLISHER: _____ YEAR _____

WHERE WAS THIS ITEM MENTIONED? _____

SECTION II: MAGAZINE/JOURNAL ARTICLE

AUTHOR: _____

ARTICLE TITLE: _____

JOURNAL TITLE: _____

VOL:_____ ISSUE: _____ DATE: _____ PAGES: _____

WHERE WAS THIS ITEM MENTIONED? _____
Required by lending library for verification.

RENEWAL REQUEST
(Please submit request 3 days before original due date.)

If possible, I would like to renew the item listed above.

You will be notified of the new due date(s) if the renewal is approved by the lending library. If it is not approved, the item(s) will be due on the original date.

Original
Due Date

Library fills in
**New
Due Date**

_____

---

for library use only

ISBN/ISSN: _____ OCLC: _____

Request Mode
Manual ☐ OCLC ☐

Lenders: _____ ILL#: _____

Date Req'd: _____ Date Rec'd:_____ DEL. TIME:_____

Due Date: _____ Date Ret'd: _____

Form revised 11/91
120 - Interlibrary Loan Forms

Estep Library   INTERLIBRARY LOAN REQUEST

Southwest Baptist University, Bolivar, MO 65613 Phone: (417) 326-1621

| PLEASE FILL IN ALL APPROPRIATE BLANKS SO REQUESTS WILL NOT BE DELAYED. STAPLE COMPUTER PRINT-OUTS TO FORM. | SBU STUDENT _____ SBU FACULTY _____ SBU STAFF _____
 SBU Off-Campus Center: Mt.Vw. _____ Spgfld. _____ Nrwd. _____
 Other SBU Off-Campus Centers: _____
 Other (please specify):_____ |

Name:_____   Phone #: _____
      (person requesting the material) PLEASE WRITE CLEARLY

Department or Course Material Will Be Used For: _____
(leave course or department name off only if request is for personal use not related to a course)

	B O O K
Book Title: _____	
Author(s): _____	
Copyright Date: _____ Publisher/Place: _____	

	A R T I C L E
Periodical Title: _____	
Title of Article: _____	
Volume: ____ Number: ____ Date of Publication: _____ Page(s): ____	

INDEX/SOURCE WHERE MATERIAL WAS FOUND:_____

LATEST DATE MATERIAL CAN BE USED: _____

You must be willing to pay postage. Photocopy charges are $.10 per page <u>or more</u>, depending on the charges where the copy is made. In addition to photocopy coast, some libraries charge a handling fee of $1.00 <u>or more</u> for interlibrary loans. Knowing this, indicate here how much your are willing to pay for your loan:_____.

<u>PLEASE allow 10 days or longer</u> for the loan to go through. You will be notified upon our receipt of the material. You may then pick up the material and pay any charges at the circulation desk.

I understand that Estep Library does not charge a sevice charge for attempting to locate the material. However, I agree to pay the lending library's charge upon receipt of my materials, even if I no longer need that material. Materials not picked up will be charged to my account with an additional $2.00 processing fee.

WARNING: If a user makes a request for, or later uses, a photocopy or reproduction for purposes in excess of "fair use," that user may be liable for copyright infringement. This institution reserves the right to refuse to accept a copy order if, in its judgement, fulfillment of the order would involve violation of the copyright law.

Signature of person making request: _____

Signature (and date) of Library Staff Receiving Form:_____ __-__-__

Interlibrary Loan Forms - 121

I.L.L. FAX REQUEST

I cannot wait the seven + days needed to receive this article through the mail. Therefore, I am willing to pay the telefacsimilie charges to receive the article sooner. I agree to pay $.10 per page plus the charges of the lending library.

Signed: _____

Staff Signature: _____

For Office Use Only Below This Line

Time Request Was Received: _____ a.m. p.m.   Date Received: _____

☐ LePac: _____

☐ OCLC: _____

LePac	OCLC	FAX Number	Charges	Confirmed?
____	____	_____	_____	yes no
____	____	_____	_____	yes no
____	____	_____	_____	yes no

Notes:

Date/Time Transmission Received: _____ - _____ - _____   _____ a.m. p.m.

Notified: yes___   no___

MARIAN LIBRARY
Book/Misc. Publication Interlibrary Loan Request

Daemon College
Amherst, New York

MPLETE ALL FOUR STEPS

EP 1   Did you look in the Marian Library Card Catalog?   Yes _____   No _____

EP 2   Identify the BOOK/PUBLICATION you are requesting:

ase

nt   AUTHOR _____

   TITLE _____

   PUBLISHER _____

   DATE/EDITION _____ ISBN _____
                                                        (If Available)

EP 3   Identify the SOURCE where you found this book/publication listed. (eg. Bibliography, index, database,
ase   etc.)
nt
   _____
                            (Title of Source)

   _____   _____   _____   _____
      (Vol.)   (Date)   (Page)   (Abstract No.)

EP 4 Your Name _____

   Address _____

   City _____ State _____ Zip _____

   Telephone No./Extention _____

   Today's Date _____

   I need this request filled by _____

   If there is a charge, I will pay up to $ _____

FOR LIBRARY USE ONLY

ILL NO _____ COMPLETED _____

Lending String _____

Lilly Library
Earlham College
Richmond, Indiana

INTERLIBRARY LOAN APPLICATION: BOOK OR THESIS
The Earlham Libraries should be used effectively before requesting an interlibrary loan.

What is your topic? _____

What course is this for? _____

IL: _____
Date: _____
Rec: _____
Due: _____
Ret: _____
R. Req.: _____
N. Date: _____

This card must be signed by the reference librarian who helped with your search. _____

Please PRINT the Following:

Author's Last Name	_First Name_	_Middle Names or Initials_

Complete Title

Place of Publication	_Publisher_	_Year_

Source where you found this book cited—Author and Title/Periodical, Volume—Page Number.
(Material will not be searched for unless line above is completed)

After what date will this book not be useful? _____

Borrower	_Box Number or Address_	_Phone_

124 - Interlibrary Loan Forms

INCARNATE WORD COLLEGE LIBRARY
Interlibrary Loan
BOOK REQUEST

Saint Pius X Library
Incarnate Word College
San Antonio, Texas

MPLETE ONE FORM PER REQUEST. PLEASE PRINT LEGIBLY.

ME_____ TODAY'S DATE_____

DRESS_____ PHONE(HM)_____ (WK)_____

CIAL SECURITY NUMBER_____

____ STUDENT _____ FACULTY (_____Dept.) _____ ADMINISTRATION _____ STAFF(_____Dept.)

ST POSSIBLE DAY YOU CAN USE MATERIAL: _____ END OF SEMESTER _____OTHER (_____).

narges are assessed by the lending library for the materials you have requested, what is the maximum amount per item you are
ing to pay?

- I will pay up to _____ $0 _____ $5.00 _____ $10.00 _____ Other ($_____)

- If you have not indicated a price limit on this form, we will assume NO LIMIT!

QUESTOR'S SIGNATURE_____

BOOK INFORMATION

AUTHOR_____

TITLE_____

_____

PUBLISHER_____ DATE OF PUBLICATION_____

THIS EDITION ONLY (·) yes · ( )no   ISBN #_____

WHERE DID YOU FIND THIS INFORMATION CITED?_____

FOR LIBRARY USE ONLY

WC catalog shows that we own this item but is: _____LOST _____checked-out.

CORAL Libraries listed as owning_____

OCLC_____
ISBN_____
DATE_____
DATE Material Rec'd_____
DUE DATE_____
RETURN DATE_____

BRARIAN'S SIGNATURE:_____

ILLFORM-1193

Interlibrary Loan Forms - 125

Reeves Memorial Library
Seton Hill College
Greensburg, Pennsylvania

Ask about
an interlibrary loan.

Books

AUTHOR _____

TITLE _____

_____

DATE OF PUBLICATION _____   PLACE _____

PUBLISHER _____.

DATE REQUESTED _____

NEEDED BEFORE _____

NAME _____

BOX NO. _____   OR PHONE _____

STATUS:
_____ SHC STUDENT _____ FACULTY _____ADMINISTRATION
_____ STAFF   _____ OTHER (specify) _____

PLEASE NOTE:

    There is a limit of 10 free book requests per
semester for SHC students, alumni, or any members of
the faculty, administration or staff. Requests above
this limit will be billed at $4.00 per request. All
patrons not associated with the college will be charged
a $4.00 processing fee per request.

LOCATIONS _____

DATE ORDERED _____   BY _____

F. W. Olin Library
Mills College
Oakland, California

Mills College Library
Interlibrary Loan Request
Periodical

Please fill in ALL spaces and PRINT clearly:

Title of Periodical: _____

Volume: _____ Issue Number: _____ Date of Issue: _____

Inclusive pages _____ to _____

Author of Article: _____

Title of Article: _____

International Standard Serial Number (ISSN): _____

NOTE:
- It may take 2 or more weeks to obtain this item.
  After which date can you no longer use it?: _____
- Many libraries charge for Interlibrary Loans, particularly university
  libraries. Charges typically range from $5.00 - $15.00.
  What is the **maximum amount** you will pay for this item?: _____
- Once an ILL transaction has begun, it is expected that the patron will
  pay for charges incurred, regardless of the date of receipt of the item.

Name: _____

Local Address: _____

Phone number: _____ Faculty Staff Student Grad

READ AND SIGN REVERSE→→→→→→→→→→→→→→→→

Return form to Susan Anderson at the Circulation Desk.

Library use only:
Verified in : _____ Borrowed from: _____
OCLC#: _____ ILL trans #: _____

F. W. Olin Library
Mills College
Oakland, California

<u>NOTICE</u>

WARNING CONCERNING COPYRIGHT RESTRICTIONS

The copyright law of the United States (Title 17, United States Code) governs the making of photocopies or other reproductions of copyrighted material.

Under certain conditions specified in the law, libraries and archives are authorized to furnish a photocopy or other reproduction. One of these specified conditions is that the photocopy or reproduction is not to be "used for any purpose other than private study, scholarship or research." If a user makes a request for, or later uses, a photocopy or reproduction for purposes in excess for "fair use," that user may be liable for copyright infringement.

This institution reserves the right to refuse to accept a copying order if, in its judgment, fulfillment of the order would involve violation of copyright law.

I agree to abide by regulations specified by both the borrowing and the lending library concerning the use of the borrowed item(s), and I promise to return the material to the Circulation Desk within the allotted time. I agree to observe copyright provisions in the use of any material requested.

X _____
(Signature of requestor)

Ask about
an interlibrary loan.

MAGAZINES

TITLE OF JOURNAL _____

VOLUME _____ NUMBER ___·___ DATE _____ PAGES _____

AUTHOR OF ARTICLE _____

TITLE OF ARTICLE _____

_____

DATE REQUESTED _____

NEEDED BEFORE _____

NAME _____

BOX NO. _____ OR PHONE _____

STATUS:
_____ SHC STUDENT _____ FACULTY _____ ADMINISTRATION
_____ STAFF _____ OTHER (specify) _____

PLEASE NOTE:

There is usually a photocopying charge for a
journal article, ranging from $1.00 to $10.00. You
will be responsible for this charge. Please specify
the maximum amount that you are willing to pay for
this article: $_____

LOCATIONS _____

DATE ORDERED _____ BY _____

Estep Library
Southwest Baptist University
Bolivar, Missouri

2-16-92

FREE PERIODICAL INTERLIBRARY LOAN REQUEST

This Does Not Apply to Periodicals for Which We Have A Current Subscription

I certify that the following article is important for my research and/or paper in:

Course Title: _____

Author(s): _____

Title of Article: _____

_____

Periodical Title (DO NOT ABBREVIATE and If you used MedLine, attach the computer printout to the to the back of this form):

_____

Volume (#):_____ No.(#):_____ Date:_____ Pages:_____

Reference was found in (index or other source name)_____

Latest date material can be used:_____

Student Signature (must be legible):_____ Phone:_____

Faculty Signature (that article is needed for student's coursework):_____

Librarian Signature (student has examined and used SBU library materials): _____
RETURN THIS FORM TO A LIBRARIAN OR A LIBRARY STAFF MEMBER. TO AVOID DELAYS, DO NOT LEAVE THIS WITH A STUDENT WORKER.

Fill out this section only if you wish to have the article faxed.

I cannot wait the seven + days needed to receive this article through the mail.
Therefore, I am willing to pay the telefacsimilie charges to receive the fax article.
I agree to pay $.10 per page plus the charges of the lending library.
SIGNED: _____ DATE:_____

WARNING: If a user makes a request for, or later uses, a photocopy or reproduction for purposes in excess of "fair use," that user may be liable for copyright infringement. This institution reserves the right to refuse to accept a copy order if, in its judgement, fulfillment of the order would involve violation of copyright law.

YOU MUST STAPLE YOUR COMPUTER PRINTOUT TO THE BACK OF THIS FORM

130 - Interlibrary Loan Forms

Babson Library
Springfield College
Springfield, Massachusetts

BABSON LIBRARY — SPRINGFIELD COLLEGE — INTERLIBRARY LOAN REQUEST

P E R I O D I C A L   R E Q U E S T   F O R M

RE WE CAN CONTACT YOU:

DATE OF REQUEST: _____

R NAME: _____ TELEPHONE NO. _____

RESS (or College Box Number): _____

k One: ☐ Grad Student ☐ Faculty ☐ Admin. ☐ Visiting Scholar

R REQUEST (Do Not Abbreviate Any Information – Print Clearly):

OR OF ARTICLE:

CLE TITLE:

RNAL NAME:

VOL.: _____ NO.: _____ DATE: _____ PAGES: _____

RCE OF REFERENCE:
e You Found Article)

mum cost you are willing to pay for copy: $

ASE READ COPYRIGHT NOTICE AT REFERENCE DESK AND SIGN BELOW (Unsigned requests cannot be processed)

ve read the *Warning Concerning Copyright Restrictions.* I accept responsibility for the above listed material's use and for any
ges and fees that accompany its acquisition even if materials arrive after my deadline, or if Babson Library is unable to anticipate
ost before request is sent."

R SIGNATURE: _____

Babson Library
Springfield College
Springfield, Massachusetts

GUIDE TO ESTIMATE CHARGES FOR ILL PHOTOCOPY REQUESTS

All Interlibrary Loan charges are based on fees charged to us by other libraries and/or vendors. Libraries with cooperative arrangements have been made by Babson Library are usually not subject to any charges.

Fees charged for article photocopies or book loans may change without notice, depending on rates determined by libraries or vendors. Charges listed below are intended only as a guide for students/faculty to estimate costs for s materials. All charges are based on an average 1-20 page article. Longer articles may incur a larger fee.

For any request, allow a minimum of 2-3 weeks for delivery of material.

If title is listed in CLGS (Cooperating Libraries of Greater Springfield) Union List – blue book at Reference Desk	NO CHARGE
If title is listed in PVULS (Pioneer Valley Union List of Serials)	ASSUME $4 MINIMUM CHARGE
If title is listed in other Union Lists (available on microfiche at the Reference Desk)	ASSUME $4 - $6 MINIMUM CHARGE
If title is a medical journal not available from above sources	ASSUME $8 - $10 MINIMUM CHARGE
If title is available only from a vednor (such as SIRC - Sport Discus)	ASSUME $10 MINIMUM CHARGE
If title is a dissertation (relatively few libraries loan copies of their dissertations)	$25 — MICROFICHE COPY $31 — PAPER COPY

INTERLIBRARY LOAN - REQUESTS FOR PERIODICAL ARTICLES

Interlibrary loan requests may be made only for periodical
articles that the library does NOT own. Once you have found a
citation for an article that interests you, please check the
FPC Periodical Holdings list BEFORE making an interlibrary
loan request. Copies of this list are available in the index
area on the second floor, and at the circulation desk.

Filling an interlibrary loan request can take ten days to two
weeks, and sometimes longer. If you have less than two weeks
before your assignment is due, please do not use the interlibrary
loan system.

FPC interlibrary loan request cards are available at the circulation desk. The request card for periodical articles
is YELLOW, and looks like this:

```
                    ILL PERIODICAL REQUEST
   REQ DATE:_____           MAXCOST_____
   NAME:_____P.O. BOX_____

   ARTICLE TITLE_____
   _____
   _____

   AUTHOR:_____

   COMPLETE JOURNAL TITLE:_____

   VOL._____NO._____DATE_____PAGES_____

   CITED IN_____CODEN_____.
                    FOR OFFICE USE ONLY
   ++++++++++++++++++++++++++++++++++++++++++++++++++++++++++
   ISSN:_____ILL NO._____OCLC NO._____

   LENDERS_____RECEIVED_____
```

HOW TO COMPLETE A REQUEST CARD

In order for an interlibrary loan request to be processed,
ALL sections of the form above the line must be completed, with
the exception of the CODEN and sometimes either the VOL. or NO.
areas. Failure to complete one of the required sections will cause
your card to be returned and will delay your request. In filling
out a request card, please follow the instructions below, and
PLEASE PRINT; illegible requests cannot be processed.

REQ DATE : Fill in the date of your request.

MAX COST : FPC belongs to a network of libraries that do not
           charge each other for photocopies provided through
           interlibrary loan. Occasionally, however, it is
           necessary for us to go outside this network to
           obtain a particular article. In this case, there
           may be a charge for the material provided. Usually,
           photocopying and service charges are in the $3 to
           $10 dollar range. If you are willing to pay a
           photocopying charge, enter the maximum amount
           here. If you do NOT want to pay a charge, enter
           0. If you enter 0, we will not try to obtain

Interlibrary Loan - 133

the article outside our own network.

ARTICLE TITLE, AUTHOR, COMPLETE JOURNAL TITLE, VOLUME, NUMBER,
DATE, and PAGES:

This information can generally be found in the original citation.
If you are not sure how to read citations provided in indexes and
other materials, ask at the circulation desk for the hand-out
on reading bibliographic citations.

COMPLETE JOURNAL TITLE: Do NOT provide abbreviated titles. Every
index has a key which provides the complete title of each journal
indexed. This title must be written out on each request.

VOLUME and NUMBER: Remember that not every citation provides both
volume number (VOL.) and issue number (NO.). Many indexes, among
them READERS' GUIDE and BUSINESS PERIODICALS INDEX, provide only
volume numbers as a general rule. If you do not have one of the
two numbers in your citation, enter a dash to indicate this.

CITED IN: For periodical article requests, this section MUST be
filled in.   Feel free to abbreviate the titles of standard
indexes, for example, RG for READERS' GUIDE, BPI for BUSINESS
PERIODICALS INDEX, and MI for the MAGAZINE INDEX.

CODEN: Only those using Biological Abstracts need provide
CODEN identifiers. These can be obtained from SERIAL
SOURCES FOR THE BIOSIS DATABASE, shelved with Biological
Abstracts. If you have a question about this, please
ask at the circulation desk.

PLEASE NOTE : Requests for articles on interlibrary loan should
made to SUPPLEMENT materials from the FPC library.
The system is NOT designed to be the main source
of research material on any particular topic, and
large numbers of requests can cause the entire
process to slow down. Please investigate the FPC
periodical collection carefully using more than
one index before ordering materials on interlibrary loan. Then, select your interlibrary loan
requests carefully.

We do not recommend that you make more than three
requests at a time. If you feel that you MUST
make more than three requests, please number all
cards consecutively in the upper left-hand
corners, assigning lower numbers to the most important articles. We will try to order as many
articles as possible; but we cannot guarantee that
all requests will be put on the system.

I.L.L. BOOK RENEWAL

Please submit this form to the I.L.L. office <u>no more than five days</u> <u>before</u> but <u>no later than 24 hours before</u> the actual due date.

BORROWER'S NAME_____
              (last)   (first)

AUTHOR_____
          (last)   (first)

TITLE_____

CURRENT DUE DATE_____

Burke Library
Hamilton College
Clinton, New York

Interlibrary Loan

Date: _____

Call Number: _____

Author: _____

Title: _____

This item is available for you on the Hold Shelf at the Circulation Desk in the Burke Library.

Please present this card when picking up material.

Please note the following restrictions:

_____

_____

_____

Interlibrary Loan

Renewal Request

Date: _____

Author: _____

Title: _____

IL#: _____

This item was requested to be renewed. lending library responded as follows:

_____

_____

_____

Interlibrary Loan

_____

:losed request is available in the
es at the following location.

umber: _____

_____ current periodical shelves

_____ 1st Floor bound periodicals

_____ 2nd Floor bound periodicals

_____ Microforms

_____ Science Library

_____ Media Library

_____ Record Library

Interlibrary Loan

Student Overdue Book

The item listed on this card was due _____

Please return it immediately to avoid a fine at the
rate of $5.00 per day. If you still need to use this
item, we can order another copy from a different
library.

L. A. Beeghley Library
Ohio Wesleyan University
Delaware, Ohio

INTERLIBRARY LOAN - PATRON RESPONSE FORM
(Interlibrary Loan Office extension is 3239)

Date:_____

Concerning your request for the following item:

_____ 1. That book is owned by the OWU libraries. It has been retrieved from the stacks and is ON HOLD for you at the Circulation desk. In the future, please be sure to check OWU holdings before placing an interlibrary loan request.

_____ 2. That book is owned by the OWU libraries. It is part of the Reference collection, however, and cannot be checked out. Please stop in and have a Reference librarian assist you.

_____ 3. That book is owned by the OWU libraries, but it is currently checked out. Please check with one of the Circulation desk staff to find out about having a RECALL placed on the item.

_____ 4. That book is too new to find out which library owns it. We suggest you try again in three months.

_____ 5. We have been unable to identify your request using the abbreviation(s) you supplied us with. Please supply complete information.

_____ 6. We have been unable to verify the request from the information given in your citation. Please supply further information or bring in your written source of reference. We will attempt again to verify the request.

_____ 7. A library that perhaps can supply this material has let us know that the citation is incorrect and that the material cannot be located as cited. Please recheck your citation.

_____ 8. The dissertation you requested is available only by purchase from University Microfilms International (UMI). If you are interested in purchasing a copy of the dissertation you requested, UMI order forms are available in the Interlibrary Loan office.

_____ 9. Copyright law prohibits us from obtaining a photocopy of the material requested. Please contact the Interlibrary Loan office to see what other options you might have.

_____ 10. Sorry, we were unable to supply your request before the deadline you indicated on your request form. If, in fact, you have more time for us to try again, please contact the Interlibrary Loan office.

_____ Other: _____

_____

_____

_____

_____

_____

138 - Interlibrary Loan Forms

Borrower

Due Date

ILL #

Please keep this bookmark with the book.

Interlibrary Loan is a privilege extended by the lending library.

Materials must be returned promptly.

Overdues may result in a loss of borrowing privileges. Please return by the date indicated to avoid fines.

The overdue charge for Interlibrary Loan items is $2.00 per day up to $10.00.

Requests for renewals should be made at least 3 days before due date.

Use the convenient form provided on the blue notification sheet or request a renewal form at the Reference Desk.

Occidental College Library
Interlibrary Loan
1600 Campus Drive
Los Angeles, CA 90041
(213) 259-2919

Interlibrary
Loan

WE HAVE BORROWED THIS BOOK FROM
ANOTHER LIBRARY FOR YOUR USE.

PLEASE RETURN THIS BOOK TO THE
WILLAMETTE UNIVERSITY LIBRARY
BY:

_____

DATE DUE

REQUEST FOR RENEWAL MUST BE
PLACED BY: _____

RENEWALS AFTER THIS DATE MAY
NOT BE POSSIBLE!

_____

BORROWER'S NAME

_____

BOX NUMBER

OVERDUE BOOKS MAY BE SUBJECT TO FINES

THIS FORM

PLEASE DO NOT REMOVE